The Spiritual World of Jezebel and Elijah

Biblical Background to the Novel
Jezebel: Harlot Queen of Israel
By Brian Godawa

The Spiritual World of Jezebel and Elijah: Biblical Background to the Novel
Jezebel: Harlot Queen of Israel
1st Edition

Copyright © 2019 Brian Godawa

All rights reserved. No part of this book may be reproduced in any form or by any electronic or mechanical means, including information storage and retrieval systems, without prior written permission, except in the case of brief quotations in critical articles and reviews.

Embedded Pictures Publishing
Los Angeles, CA
brian@embeddedpictures.com
www.embeddedpictures.com

ISBN: 978-1-942858-46-1 (paperback)
ISBN: 978-1-942858-47-8 (ebook)

Scripture quotations taken from *The Holy Bible: English Standard Version*. Wheaton: Standard Bible Society, 2001.

Get the novel *Jezebel* that is based on the biblical research of this book you are reading.

The Most Ruthless Queen in Ancient Israel.

Israel thought she was bringing unity, progress, and change. She brought Baal, the storm god of Canaan.

https://godawa.com/get-jezebel/

(*This is an affiliate link. I get a commission on it.*)

Table of Contents

Get the Novel Jezebel iii
Table of Contents iv
Chapter 1: The Characters 1
   Jezebel 1
   Installation of the High Priestess 9
   Elijah 10
   Jehu 14
   Athaliah 18
   The Rechabites 20
Chapter 2: The Spiritual World of Israel 25
   Monotheist or Polytheist? 25
   The Watchers 33
   1 Kings 22 38
   Leviathan 40
Chapter 3: The Gods of Canaan 45
   Baal 45
   The Image of Baal 49
   The Temple of Baal 50
   Yahweh Versus Baal 52
   Asherah 54
   Astarte 59
   Anat 61
   Mot 64
   Molech 69
   The Archangels 72
Chapter 4: Cosmic Geography 76
   Underworld Valleys 76
   Sheol 81
   Cosmic Mountains 86
Chapter 5: Cultic Practice 94
   High Places 94
   Standing Stones 96
   Masks 98
   Qedeshim 99
   Sacred Marriage 102
   Family Shrines 105
   Cult of the Dead 107
   Marzeah Feast 111
   Rephaim 115
   Child Sacrifice 123
Great Offers By Brian Godawa 138
About the Author 139

I receive commissions on all links to Amazon books in this book.

Chapter 1:
The Characters

The Story First

Many of my readers like to learn about the biblical and historical research behind my novels after they've read them. The fact behind the fiction. It helps bring context and explains some of the "stranger things" of the novels to those who are intellectually and spiritually curious. This book is a presentation of the research behind my novel *Jezebel: Harlot Queen of Israel*. The truth is that the material in this book is so fascinating it can be read on its own by those who hunger as I do to uncover the ancient Near Eastern background of the biblical text.

The novel retells the biblical story centered around Queen Jezebel of Israel that can be found in 1 Kings 16 through 2 Kings 11. Jezebel, a daughter of the king of Tyre, marries King Ahab of Israel in the ninth century B.C. The marriage is a political one for the purposes of uniting in defense against the hostile Aramean kingdom in the north. Despite the pragmatism, king and queen find themselves falling in love.

Tyre, a Phoenician coastal city, is cosmopolitan and Canaanite. So Jezebel brings wealth, sophistication, and culture to a less advanced agrarian Israel. Unfortunately, she also brings the worship of Baal, the storm god of Canaan, and even builds a temple to him in Samaria, the heart of Israel.

Since Israel is supposed to be monotheist in its worship of Yahweh alone, the prophet Elijah the Tishbite and his students at the School of Prophets rise up to condemn Jezebel and call Ahab and Israel back to Yahweh from their spiritual adultery with Baal. This leads to a series of confrontations between the two worldviews that play out in the narrative, the most famous of which is the Mount Carmel episode of calling fire down from heaven.

But Jezebel doesn't give up. She fights back to gain more power and even trains Ahab's sister Athaliah to emulate her ways as future queen down in Judah. Jezebel's ruthless ambition forces a climactic battle that jeopardizes an entire family dynasty of kings.

The story of the novel is told through the eyes of Jehu son of Nimshi, who is the commander of the army of Israel. Jehu is a man who struggles with dual loyalty to both God and King. His dilemma becomes more pressing as the king whom Yahweh anointed strays from his God. As Jezebel's power grows, Jehu must rise up to do what is right, facing the loss of everything he holds dear, or suffer the damning consequences of doing nothing.

Another unique aspect of the novel is the depiction of the spiritual world. As I will explain in Chapter 2, the novel pulls back the curtain of the unseen realm. It depicts the "spiritual principalities and powers" that reign behind pagan Gentile nations and how they have influence on the course of history. Baal, Asherah, Molech, and others are not mere myths without bite. They are actual names of demonic powers that are real and have their own agenda.

Though this is obviously speculative, the principle is biblical. This is not simplistic "spiritual warfare" of demons of lust and gossip clinging to us like bacterial ghosts of influence. This is the bigger picture of higher entities of power ruling over Gentile nations as depicted in Deuteronomy 32:8-10 and Psalm 82. Nevertheless, the storyline of these spiritual powers is intended to reflect the mythology of pagans and how it reflects spiritual reality within a biblical worldview.

Thus, as Jezebel seeks to implant Baal worship in Israel, we see the spiritual entity named Baal and his allies, Astarte, Asherah, Anat, and others maneuver for power in the spiritual territories of Israel and Judah, much like human mobsters might maneuver for power over their regions in a city under their control.

But Yahweh and his archangels have other plans to protect the seed of David from the Seed of the Serpent. That is the basic storyline of the novel *Jezebel: Harlot Queen of Israel*. Now enjoy learning about the historical and biblical research behind it all.

The Spiritual World of Jezebel and Elijah

Jezebel

The story of Jezebel and Elijah is one of the most exciting and iconic narratives in all the Bible. One of the most well-known biblical miracles was Elijah's showdown with Jezebel's prophets of Baal on Mount Carmel. Considered the most wicked queen in Israel's history, Jezebel has become a symbol for some in the modern church of women who embrace feminism. Feminists have sought to rehabilitate her image by revising it into one of a strong female misunderstood and oppressed by the "patriarchy." Some prophecy pundits even believe we are currently reliving her storyline as end times prophecy.

Regardless of what you think of these various reactions, Queen Jezebel and the prophet Elijah remain as relevant to us today as they were 2,900 years ago.

In the novel, I have sought to depict Jezebel fairly and faithfully within her original ancient Near Eastern context. That context included both the volatile world of the divided kingdoms of ninth-century Israel and Judah—the prophet Elijah's people as well as the culturally influential cosmopolitan spirit of Phoenicia—Jezebel's homeland. My research involved fascinating Bible scholarship, archaeology, and Canaanite mythology that I just had to share with my readers.

Let's start with the queen bee, herself.

One of the first things the reader will notice is that the name of Jezebel in the story is actually Izabel, an anglicized version of her real Sidonian name, Ai-zebul. The Hebrew name change from Izabel to Jezebel is not merely a matter of dialect difference but a form of ancient prophetic insult. Ai-zebul (Izabel) translated most likely meant "Where is the Prince?"[1] This was the phrase Baal worshippers would utter every harvest as they waited for their crops to arrive. It was symbolized in their myth of Baal, the god of storm and vegetation, being rescued from death in the underworld, who would then bring life back to their fields. Hillel Millgram explains,

---

[1] G. Mussies, "Jezebel," ed. Karel van der Toorn, Bob Becking, and Pieter W. van der Horst, *Dictionary of Deities and Demons in the Bible* (Leiden; Boston; Köln; Grand Rapids, MI; Cambridge: Brill; Eerdmans, 1999), 473.

This myth, the centerpiece of Canaanite religion, found expression in Canaanite liturgy. During summer, the time of Baal's long absence, the worshipers of Baal would go out in procession "seeking Baal," chanting: "Where is Baal the Conqueror? Where is the Prince, the Lord of the Earth?" With the coming of the rains in the autumn, the cry would go up: "Baal the Conqueror lives! The Prince of the Earth has revived!" By their very names, Ethbaal and his daughter Jezebel proclaim the central beliefs of their religion. Ethbaal (its Phoenician form is Ittobaal) means "Baal Exists!" It is a proclamation of faith.[2]

Though Ethbaal and his daughter were priests of Astarte, their names carried the name of their most high god, Baal, a common naming technique of the ancient Near East, including Israel. In that world, names were also believed to assign destinies and even became expressions of authority by the namer over the named.[3] Thus Abram's name, which meant "exalted father," was changed by God to Abraham, which meant "father of many nations" (Genesis 17:5) because that is what God would make him in his future.

In Jezebel's case, the text of 1 and 2 Kings renames Ai-zebul to Ee-zebel (Jezebel in English), which linguistically in Hebrew turns her name into a profanity of excrement. Millgram again explains,

> First *Ai* (where) was changed to *Ee*, a negative (none); thus Ai-Zebul (Where is the Prince? Where is the Exalted One?) becomes Ee-Zebul, "There is no Prince," or "Unexalted." Then Zebul (Prince, Exalted One) was altered to Zebel (feces, excrement).[4]

This named future of Jezebel is expressed in 2 Kings 9:37, which reduces the powerful queen to pathos with a double entendre of her future demise: "And the corpse of Jezebel shall be as dung on the face of the field in the

---

[2] Millgram, Hillel I., *The Elijah Enigma* (K Locations 1106-1117). McFarland & Company, Inc., Publishers. K Edition.
[3] John H Walton, Zondervan *Illustrated Bible Backgrounds Commentary (Old Testament): Genesis, Exodus, Leviticus, Numbers, Deuteronomy, vol. 1* (Grand Rapids, MI: Zondervan, 2009), 31–32.
[4] Millgram, Hillel I., *The Elijah Enigma* (K Locations 1266-1273). McFarland & Company, Inc., Publishers. K Edition.

territory of Jezreel, so that no one can say, 'This is Jezebel.'" The question her name was based upon, "Where is the prince (Baal)?" is related to his return from death to bring the rains and harvest. Just like no one can say, "Here is Baal," because he is not the true storm god, so no one will be able to say "here is Jezebel." Like her humbled god, she will be permanently shamefully reduced to dung on the field that awaits the rains from the true storm god, Yahweh.

This same technique of renaming is used elsewhere in the Bible. Another example I used in the novel was that of Ashtoreth, a goddess who shows up often in the Old Testament.[5] The name refers to the infamous Astarte (Phoenician: Ashtart) of Canaan and was in fact the goddess whom Jezebel's father served as high priest.[6]

It is said that ignoring someone is the most vicious way to hurt them. False gods were bad enough to the ancient Hebrew, but female goddesses were so offensive that the Bible writers didn't use a word for goddess. They simply used their names (Asherah, Ashtoreth, Lilith).[7] But it has long been noted that the name Ashtoreth was a deliberate diabolical distortion of Astarte by using the vowels of the Hebrew word for "shame" (*bosheth*) between the consonants of Astarte.[8] The goddess was too shameful or profane for Hebrews to use her real name.

Names and language are powerful tools for altering our interpretation of reality. I've explained more extensively how God and the writers of the Bible altered, subverted, reimagined, and deconstructed pagan imagination and concepts in my book *God Against the gods: Storytelling, Imagination, and Apologetics in the Bible.* (Affiliate link)

But this doesn't exhaust the biblical usage of Jezebel's name for theological purposes. In the New Testament book of Revelation, Jezebel

---

[5] See 1King 11:15, 33; 2King 23:13; 1Sam 31:10.

[6] Josephus, *Against Apion* 1.18.

[7] In all my Chronicles series of novels, I make the fallen Watchers pose as the gods of the nations. Since angelic beings in the Bible are all male in gender, I have the Watchers masquerading as women goddesses.

[8] John Day, *Yahweh and the Gods and Goddesses of Canaan (The Library of Hebrew Bible/Old Testament Studies)* (Bloomsbury T&T Clark, 2002), 214.

shows up as a metaphor for spiritual apostasy among God's people. In Christ's message to the seven churches of Asia Minor, he warns the church at Thyatira of a "Jezebel."

> Revelation 2:18–23:
> But I have this against you, that you tolerate that woman Jezebel, who calls herself a prophetess and is teaching and seducing my servants to practice sexual immorality and to eat food sacrificed to idols. I gave her time to repent, but she refuses to repent of her sexual immorality. Behold, I will throw her onto a sickbed, and those who commit adultery with her I will throw into great tribulation, unless they repent of her works, and I will strike her children dead.

This condemnation has led to the common image of Jezebel as a harlot or sexually immoral woman. Some modern Christians call women who are sexually active outside of marriage "Jezebels." But a closer look at the context reveals that this is not really the apostolic intent of the imagery.

While it is possible the false teaching in Thyatira may have included sexual rituals, since pagan religions often did, it isn't likely this is the import of the text here. Christ was drawing from the books of 1 and 2 Kings as an analogy for what was going on in the Church. Jezebel wasn't criticized in the Old Testament for engaging in sexual immorality. She was damned for bringing Baal worship to Israel.

When Jezebel is first introduced in 1 Kings 16:31-33, she is described as the wife of Ahab who influenced him to build a temple of Baal and worship the Canaanite god, along with Asherah. And in Ahab's obituary in 1 Kings 21:25-26, it was said of him that "there was none who sold himself to do what was evil in the sight of the LORD like Ahab, whom Jezebel his wife incited" to go after abominable idols. But there is no mention of any sexual sin against her husband.

Jezebel could very likely have been a faithful, loving wife to Ahab. That is why she is portrayed as such in the novel. At least, she starts out that way. Her evil was not sexual immorality. Rather, sexual immorality was a metaphor for her spiritual evil of making Baal worship more popular in Israel.

The Spiritual World of Jezebel and Elijah

Israel was called Yahweh's bride throughout the Old Testament.[9] His relationship with his people was so sacred and intimate that it was covenanted like a marriage. So when Israel worshipped other gods like Baal, Asherah, Molech, and others, the prophets all likened that apostasy to marital unfaithfulness to her husband Yahweh. The most recurring image used of Israel in prophetic denunciations by God was that of an unfaithful wife, described as a harlot, adulteress, or prostitute.[10]

Israel's spiritual infidelity was so prevalent that the prophets Isaiah and Jeremiah described her as "playing the whore," having sex with idols from the nations, "on every high hill and under every green tree" (Isaiah 57:5; Jeremiah 2:20; 3:6-9), which were the locations of the forbidden high places of idol worship. Ezekiel likened Judah's polytheism to a spiritual prostitute "offering herself" sexually "to any passerby," the gods of the Egyptians, Philistines, Assyrians, and Babylonians (Ezekiel 16:24-29, 35-36).

The Jezebel of Revelation was a *religious and spiritual* "whore" because of her apostate teachings as a so-called prophetess. Christians following those teachings were likened to "committing adultery with her." There is even reason to believe that the Jezebel of Revelation 2 is poetically linked to the "Great Harlot" who rides the scarlet Beast of Revelation 17.

The first step in understanding this connection is to realize that of the seven churches in Revelation 2-3, Thyatira is the fourth, which places it exactly in the middle of the seven. A well-known and oft-used literary device of many biblical writers is the poetic structure called "chiasm." In short, chiasm is the structuring of a narrative where the first half of the story builds to a midpoint climax, which represents the most important thematic focus. Then the last half of the story mirrors the first half but in reverse, as if it is undoing the tension built up to the middle.

If the seven churches sequence of Revelation is understood as a chiasm, then that spiritual prophetess and harlot Jezebel is the midpoint focal theme.

---

[9] Israel as married to Yahweh: Jeremiah 2.2; 31.32; Hosea 2:14–15; cf. 13.4–5.

[10] Israel's unfaithfulness to Yahweh described as sexual infidelity and prostitution: Hosea 2:2; Jeremiah 3:6; Exodus 34:15–16; Leviticus 17:7; Numbers 15:39; 25:1; Deuteronomy 31:16; Judges 2:17; 8:27, 33; 1Chronicles 5:25; 2Chronicles 21:11, 13; Psalm 106:39; Isaiah 1:21; Jeremiah 2:20; 3:1–9; 5:7; Ezekiel 6:9; 16:15–17, 20, 22, 25–36, 41; 23:5–8, 11, 14, 19–19, 27–30, 35, 44; 43:7, 9; Hosea 1:2, 2:2, 4–5; 3:3; 4:10–15, 18; 5:3–4; 6:10; 9:1; Joel 3:3; Amos 7:17; Micah 1:7; Nahum 3:4.

And it is precisely that royal/priestly figure of the Great Harlot, Mystery Babylon, which is being judged in Revelation 17. In fact, the judgment of that spiritually important city seems to be a climactic center point for Revelation's series of judgments (for a complete narrative story of who Mystery Babylon was, see my novel series *Chronicles of the Apocalypse – paid link*).

In conclusion, both Old and New Testaments explain Jezebel's harlotry as a spiritual analogy of apostasy, not earthly sexual behavior.

Jezebel's father was a priest of Baal, but he also became king of Tyre. So Jezebel was most likely a high priestess of Astarte since it was Phoenician custom to appoint the king's daughter as the high priestess of the local gods.[11] Astarte was considered Baal's consort in the Phoenician pantheon of Tyre. The writer of 2 Kings makes a poetic connection of Jezebel with the shameful goddess Astarte. And he does so during the description of her death at the command of Jehu, thus linking her execution with the eradication of goddess worship.

After Jehu had killed the king of Israel, he entered Jezreel to eliminate all of Ahab's family. His first order of business was to kill Jezebel. Jezebel heard that Jehu was coming, so she prepared for his arrival. The text says, "She painted her eyes and adorned her head and looked out of the window" (2 Kings 9:30). This is a peculiar thing to draw attention to in such a story. Knowing how much Jezebel and Jehu despised each other, it would be foolish of Jezebel to think she could seduce the zealous warrior king. But Jezebel was no fool. The writer is making a deliberate artistic reference to a very common motif of Astarte worship in Canaan: the "woman in the window."

Multiple ivory reliefs from the Iron Age have been found throughout Mesopotamia and the Levant that depict a woman peering out of a window.[12] She is linked to the cult of Astarte as a fertility goddess.[13] The writer of 2 Kings describes Jezebel as painting herself with make-up, a common motif of

---

[11] David Noel Freedman, "Jezebel," *The Anchor Yale Bible Dictionary* (New York: Doubleday, 1996), 848.

[12] Ivories of the Woman in the Window have been found in Arslan-Tash, Khorsabad, Nimrud and Samaria, Jezebel's second home. Eleanor Ferris Beach, "The Samaria Ivories, Marzeah, and Biblical Text," *Biblical Archaeologist* 55:3 (1992), pp. 130-139.

[13] Nehama Aschkenasy, *Woman at the Window: Biblical Tales of Oppression and Escape* (Detroit, MI: Wayne State University Press), 12.

seduction (Jeremiah 4:30), in this case the spiritual seduction by false goddesses. Jezebel was about to be attacked and destroyed just as the goddess whom she had brought to Israel was about to be attacked.

As archaeologist Eleanor Ferris Beach puts it, "In Jezebel, the literary Jehu encounters the personified visual image from the marzeah couch [Woman at the Window], and he shatters her, quite physically, as the last obstacle to the throne. He thereby denies the necessary memorial rites to the murdered kings and queen mother and asserts his independent legitimacy."[14]

The "marzeah" mentioned in the previous quotation was a ritual banquet feast that was part of a hero-cult of the dead. The marzeah memorialized the death of one king and his living replacement, who was approved by previous kings now in the underworld (more on marzeah and the cult of the dead later in this book).

Installation of the High Priestess

In the novel, Jezebel's installation as high priestess to Baal in Tyre is depicted with liturgy and fanfare. This is based on an existing manuscript of rituals from ancient Emar called *The Installation of the Storm God's High Priestess*.[15] For the sake of story pacing, I've used creative license to draw elements from the text and telescope the ceremony from nine days into a mere one day.

In the original text, day one involved anointing the priestess's head with oil and sacrificing a sheep along with a jar of barley and jug of wine. Day two was the shaving of the priestess with another sacrifice of one ox and six sheep. Here we are told of the "divine weapon" as an axe that was used as a symbolic sacred implement. The priestess was shaved at the entrance to the temple.

Day three involved more sacrifices with singers in a procession, presentation of the sacred weapon, and the high priestess's entrance into the

---

[14] Eleanor Ferris Beach, "The Samaria Ivories, Marzeah, and Biblical Text." *The Biblical Archaeologist*, Vol. 56, No. 2 (Jun., 1993), 101.

[15] Translated by Daniel Fleming, Eds., William W. Hallo and K. Lawson Younger, *The Context of Scripture* (Leiden; New York: Brill, 1997–), 427.

temple. She is described as wearing gold earrings and the gold ring of Baal while her head is wrapped with a red headdress. She is carried on the shoulders of her brothers to the house of her father, where the elders then bow before her and offer gifts of silver.

The next six days are filled with daily sacrifices of sheep and offerings of loaves, cakes, and fruit, along with goblets of wine and barley beer presented to the storm god Baal.

On the final ninth day, the priestess leaves her father's house with a veiled face like a bride and is taken to the temple of Baal, where more sacrifices are made and she offers her own sacrifice of lamb and loaves.

A large feast by the elders is followed by placing on her a fine robe. Then she is shown to her bedroom. Her feet are washed, and she lies down to sleep.

Elijah

Elijah the Tishbite is one of the most fascinating characters in the whole of Scripture. He is the first of the line of major prophets used to call Israel and Judah back to Yahweh, and he becomes so symbolically important that he was prophesied to return before Messiah would come to bring the Day of the Lord.

> Malachi 4:5:
> ⁵ Behold, I will send you Elijah the prophet before the great and awesome day of the LORD comes.

Jesus explained that John the Baptist was the fulfillment of this prophecy as a spiritual symbol rather than a physical reincarnation (Matthew 11:12-14; Mark 9:11-13, Luke 1:17). John the Baptist came "in the spirit and power of Elijah" to be the messenger announcing Messiah as well as the destruction of the old covenant temple that Messiah replaced with his new covenant (Malachi 3:1-3).

> Malachi 3:1–2:
> Behold, I send my messenger, and he will prepare the way before me. And the Lord whom you seek will suddenly come to his temple; and the messenger of the covenant in whom you delight, behold, he is coming, says the LORD of

hosts. But who can endure the day of his coming, and who can stand when he appears?

At the Mount of Transfiguration, Elijah showed up with Moses to validate Jesus as Messiah (Matthew 17:1-17). The team of Moses and Elijah had become a symbolic expression of the "Law and the Prophets," or the whole of the Scriptures. So their presence at the transfiguration was another way of God saying that all the Scriptures point to the supremacy of Jesus.

Elijah was only one of two men in Scripture who never died but were taken away to heaven. Enoch was the other. (2 Kings 2:11-12. Genesis 5:24). The story of Elijah's fiery chariot ascension is told in the novel *Jezebel: Harlot Queen of Israel.*

But perhaps one of the most endearing character traits of the prophet was his fear. I think this is why he is so relatable to most believers despite being given such a high calling and status in the family of God.

Here you have a man who does one of the most gutsy things anyone can do, call a contest of gods in the real world (1 Kings 18:17-41). He tells Ahab to bring his prophets of Baal and Asherah to Mount Carmel and to set up an altar sacrifice. And Elijah would do the same. Then they were to each call upon their gods respectively and see which god would answer with fire from heaven. The scene is emblazoned in the minds of believers as one of the most glorious miracles outside of the Red Sea deliverance and the resurrection of Christ.

So there is Elijah, having just won that contest and slaughtered four hundred prophets of Baal in a display of Yahweh's power and might. Then he gets a letter—a mere letter—from Jezebel threatening his life in return (1 Kings 19:2), and he runs like a scaredy-cat into the desert for forty days and forty nights all the way to Mount Horeb.

On the one hand, having your life threatened by a queen is no minor thing. But when it comes from the loser over whose god you've just won a major victory, you can't help but wonder how a person could fall from the heights of faith to the depths of fear so instantaneously. Or rather, how such a man of God who had experienced the power of God, unlike any of us, could be so weak in faith.

And therein lies Elijah's relatableness to us. For who hasn't wondered at their own pathetic lack of faith or easy fall into temptation? Who hasn't questioned their own relationship to God as fraudulent because of some besetting sin? It would be doubly tempting to conclude that holiness is just too difficult to achieve. That great people of God like the prophets are simply impossible examples of unattainable heroism.

But Elijah is an attainable model after all. He is one of the most important prophets in God's plan, and yet he is one of the most human—*the most like us*—precisely because he acts just like us even though he has experienced much more of God's power and glory than any of us likely ever will.

He is also similar to the Israelite nation, who after being delivered through the parting of the Red Sea, just a short time later cast and worshipped a golden calf. They just couldn't wait long enough for the ten commandments.

I find great comfort and hope in following the example of a man who, when he fled in fear, didn't just run away from evil but *ran toward his God*—at Mount Horeb, another name for Mount Sinai, the mountain of Yahweh's presence. It was faith that made Elijah run to God in his fear. We'll talk about cosmic mountains later. But my goal in exploring Elijah's character was a personal journey of struggling with trying to understand the nature of faith and fear in all of us.

Then Elijah has the experience at Sinai where he observes great miraculous spectacles of wind, earthquake, and fire and yet discerns that "God is not in" these traditionally understood means of theophany. God, it turns out, speaks to him instead in "a still small voice" (1 Kings 19:9-12). At least that is how some have translated it. But looking more closely at the Hebrew of the text, I found that the phrase isn't really about an audible voice at all. It's more like an oxymoron, like saying "the sound of silence." *The New Interpreter's Bible* explains it this way:

> The traditional translation of the phrase as "a still small voice" (so KJV) has been popularized in hymns, but it does not convey the oxymoron. The NRSV takes it to be "a sound of sheer silence," which is what the words mean, and yet Elijah is able to hear something (v. 13)... In any case, the

structure of the text implies that it is in this stillness that
Elijah somehow encounters the Lord.[16]

It wouldn't make sense to conclude that God speaks through soft whispers or internal feelings instead of external spectacle. In fact, that would contradict the Bible. After all, God had just spoken through the external spectacle of fire from heaven, not to mention previous spectacles of food multiplication and resurrection of the dead (1 Kings 17) with more spectacle to come (2 Kings 2). He couldn't be saying that he really didn't speak through those things.

Rather, I think the picture being painted here is more of an object lesson for Elijah's faith. Perhaps the point was more about walking by faith than by sight, for when we see spectacle, we believe. But as soon as we don't, our faith falters and we worship idols. We are a fickle lot, we humans. We tend to trust only what we can see or experience. But the Scripture's focus is on the life of faith as "the assurance of things hoped for, the conviction of things not seen" (Hebrews 11:1).

Perhaps God was using one instance where he was not in the usual theophany to draw Elijah to him through his seeming absence. It is the times in life when we are suffering or dry and don't feel God's presence, when we don't "experience" him, that we start to wonder where he is because he appears silent. It isn't that we have to calm down and listen because he's whispering, but rather *that he is in the silence itself*. It is the silence that cuts through our distractions and self-delusions and forces us to long for eternity and for our Maker. And it is in that longing of silence that we find him.

The cliché "absence makes the heart grow fonder" is quite relevant here for our character growth, even if not something some modern believers want to hear, especially those who may highly value "spiritual experiences."

Perhaps there is some truth to the mystic's claim that God's presence can be found in his "absence." Of course as infinite Creator, God is always everywhere present, so this isn't a theological proposition of God being literally absent, but more an expression of our own lack of experiencing that

---

[16] Choon-Leong Seow, "The First and Second Books of Kings," in *New Interpreter's Bible*, ed. Leander E. Keck, vol. 3 (Nashville: Abingdon Press, 1994–2004), 142.

presence. When we have that realization, we connect with God whether there is spectacle or not, in pleasure or in pain, in presence or in absence, in joy or in suffering. My attempt at translating that biblical event at Sinai in the novel was another journey of attempting to make sense of a truth through narrative that couldn't really be as effectively expressed through systematic theology.

Forgive me for quoting pop culture to conclude, but I think I now have a stronger appreciation for the words of a famous song whose lyrics many may have listened to without ever hearing the echoes of Scripture within *The Sounds of Silence* by Simon and Garfunkle.

> And the people bowed and prayed
> To the neon God they made,
> And the sign flashed out its warning
> In the words that it was forming,
> And the signs said, "The words of the prophets
> Are written on the subway walls and tenement halls,"
> And whispered in the sounds of silence.

Jehu

Jehu, son of Nimshi, is the protagonist in the novel *Jezebel: Harlot Queen of Israel*. Jehu had a peculiar relationship to heroism. Because of his extremely violent actions of killing Jezebel, killing all the house of Ahab, and deceiving the Baal priests into a trap of death, he is criticized by some scholars as being a flawed hero who went too far with his pursuit of justice. As one commentator put it: "The activities of Jehu, however, are characterized by a brutality that goes beyond reason and a religious zeal which in its results has little to commend it."[17]

This negative interpretation seems supported by one prophecy in Hosea where God tells the prophet to marry a harlot and name her first child Jezreel as a prelude to the punishment of exile that is about to happen.

---

[17] T. R. Hobbs, *2 Kings, vol. 13, Word Biblical Commentary* (Dallas: Word, Incorporated, 1998), 119.

The Spiritual World of Jezebel and Elijah

> Hosea 1:4:
> And the LORD said to him, "Call his name Jezreel, for in just a little while I will punish the house of Jehu for the blood of Jezreel, and I will put an end to the kingdom of the house of Israel."

So the idea here is that Jehu was in some way guilty for the blood he spilled when he killed Jezebel and the kings of both Judah and Israel in Jezreel (2 Kings 9). While in Jezreel, Jehu wrote to the elders of Samaria and told them to bring Jehu the heads of the sons of Ahab residing in the city (2 Kings 10). Then Jehu called all the worshippers of Baal throughout Samaria to come to the temple of Baal because Jehu was going to perform a sacrifice to Baal. Jehu said he wanted to prove that he was going to have greater devotion to the deity than even Ahab had expressed. But this was just a deception to bring all the Baal worshippers together so he could kill them all and destroy the temple of Baal (2 Kings 10:18-28).

But there is a problem here, because these very actions of Jehu were commanded by Yahweh and predicted favorably by Yahweh's prophets, so why would Jehu be condemned for doing what God told him to do?

Elijah the prophet gave the word of the Lord to Ahab himself.

> 1 Kings 21:21–24:
> Behold, I will bring disaster upon you. I will utterly burn you up, and will cut off from Ahab every male, bond or free, in Israel. ...because you have made Israel to sin. And of Jezebel the LORD also said, "The dogs shall eat Jezebel within the walls of Jezreel." Anyone belonging to Ahab who dies in the city the dogs shall eat, and anyone of his who dies in the open country the birds of the heavens shall eat."

In this passage, it is very clear from the words of God's own mouthpiece, Elijah, that Yahweh was not merely predicting Jehu's slaughter of the house of Ahab and Jezebel, but that God's own hand was in it. "I will burn you up and cut you off . . . I will make your house barren" is all language of God's own providential involvement in the killings. In this sense, Jehu's actions were Yahweh's own actions. Later, Elisha repeats the prophecy to Jehu with its justification, "so that I may avenge on Jezebel the blood of my servants the prophets, and the blood of all the servants of the LORD" (2 Kings 9:6-10). God was using Jehu *as his own hand of vengeance* to destroy the line of Ahab.

But what about the deception that Jehu used to trap and kill the Baal worshippers, what about Jehu's execution of Ahaziah, king of Judah? Those weren't mentioned in the prophecies. Were they excessive overreach by Jehu's own violent character?

The deception of Jehu bringing in the Baal worshippers is surely not an evil, since all warfare and trapping evildoers requires deception in order to lure them to justice. That kind of "deception" is universally accepted as morally justifiable. The Baal worshippers would hardly have come of their own accord to their judgment. Regarding their slaughter, it isn't inconsistent with Elijah's commands to kill the prophets of Baal on Mount Carmel (1 Kings 18:40). But God had also decreed that Jehu would be anointed by Elijah to be king of Israel whose sword would bring God's judgment upon many.

> 1 Kings 19:16–18:
> And the one who escapes from the sword of Hazael [king of Syria] shall Jehu put to death, and the one who escapes from the sword of Jehu shall Elisha put to death. Yet I will leave seven thousand in Israel, all the knees that have not bowed to Baal, and every mouth that has not kissed him.

King Hazael was the king of Syria who fought against Israel and killed many of his people. While this prophecy is not necessarily a prescriptive command, it certainly is a justification since Elisha the prophet was described as killing those who escaped Jehu's sword. And the context given here is the worship of Baal, which implicates the bloodguilt of Baal worshippers.

The only other death in need of explanation is Jehu's execution of Ahaziah, king of Judah. Though this was not commanded by Yahweh, its justification is found in the scriptural connection of Ahaziah to that house of Ahab that Jehu was justified in destroying: "[Ahaziah] also walked in the way of the house of Ahab and did what was evil in the sight of the LORD, as the house of Ahab had done, for he was son-in-law to the house of Ahab" (2 Kings 9:27).

After the text describes Jehu's actions positively as wiping out Baal from Israel, Yahweh himself gives his blessing on Jehu for "carrying out what is right in my eyes, and have done to the house of Ahab according to all that was in my heart" (2 Kings 10:30). No better approval than from God's own heart.

So, if Jehu was justified in all the blood he shed, why would Hosea speak of Jehu's bloodguilt in Jezreel? Perhaps the answer lies in the qualification right after the blessing:

> 2 Kings 10:31:
> But Jehu was not careful to walk in the law of the LORD, the God of Israel, with all his heart. He did not turn from the sins of Jeroboam, which he made Israel to sin.

Bible commentator Stuart Douglas explains that Hosea was not "condemning Jehu for fulfilling God's command. Instead, Yahweh now announces that he will turn the tables on the house of Jehu because of the real issue, i.e., *what has happened in the meantime*. In the same way that Jehu in 842 [B.C.] had annihilated a dynasty famed for its long history of oppression and apostasy, so Yahweh himself will now put an end to the Jehu dynasty because it, in turn, has grown hopelessly corrupt."[18]

Jehu has an additional historical interest because he is one of the few biblical characters who have been found on archaeological inscriptions unearthed in Israel. The Black Obelisk of Shalmaneser III contains the only known possible image of an Israelite king, and that king is Jehu. Discovered in modern day Nimrud in northern Iraq, the location of ancient Assyria of the ninth century B.C., the obelisk is about seven feet tall and is inscribed with both text and relief sculptures depicting events from Shalmaneser's reign in Assyria. As the Zondervan Illustrated Bible Backgrounds Commentary describes it:

> Among the reliefs is one that shows Jehu kneeling before the Assyrian emperor in the course of his western campaign of 841 B.C.—the only contemporary portrait in existence of an Israelite king. The relief is accompanied by the following caption: "The tribute of Jehu, son of Omri: I received from

---

[18] Douglas Stuart, *Hosea–Jonah*, vol. 31, *Word Biblical Commentary* (Dallas: Word, Incorporated, 2002), 29.

him silver, gold, a golden bowl, a golden vase with pointed bottom, golden tumblers, golden buckets, tin, a staff for a king, and javelins."[19]

The following image is by Steven G. Johnson and is licensed under the Creative Commons Attribution-Share Alike 3.0 Unported license.

Possible depiction of Jehu King of Israel giving tribute to King Shalmaneser III of Assyria, on the Black Obelisk of Shalmaneser III from Nimrud (circa 827 BC) in the British Museum (London).

Athaliah

In the novel, Athaliah is depicted as a young sister of Ahab whom Jezebel takes under her wing to prepare her for marrying the prince of Judah for political diplomacy. In the Bible, she was in fact married this way for that very purpose. But some believe she was the daughter of Ahab because the Bible seems to indicate she was.

---

[19] John H Walton, *Zondervan Illustrated Bible Backgrounds Commentary (Old Testament): 1 & 2 Kings, 1 & 2 Chronicles, Ezra, Nehemiah, Esther*, vol. 3 (Grand Rapids, MI: Zondervan, 2009), 149.

The Spiritual World of Jezebel and Elijah

Unfortunately, there are a couple problems with that theory. First, 2 Kings 8:18 describes Athaliah as the "daughter of Ahab." But just a few lines down in verse 26 of that same chapter, Athaliah is called the "daughter of Omri." I don't believe this is a contradiction because phrases about offspring like "son of" are known to be very elastic in meaning. They can mean the immediate son of someone or the distant ancestor of that same person. This is most notable in the declaration of Jesus Christ to be the "Son of David." He was in the lineage of David and as such is described as a son in a distant sense. In the same way, "daughter of" could be a reference to daughter, granddaughter, or a distant ancestral designation as in "the lineage of."

So if Athaliah was the immediate daughter of Ahab, she could be considered in the household lineage of ("daughter of") Omri, her actual grandfather. Or if she was the immediate daughter of Omri, now dead, and she was taken in by her brother Ahab and his wife Jezebel, then she could be referred to as both a daughter of Omri and of Ahab. So is she the immediate daughter of Ahab or Omri?

Scholar H.J. Katzenstein has provided a solution. In his aptly titled article "Who Were the Parents of Athaliah?", he writes that by synchronizing with known dates of Assyrian kings and other scholarly references, we are able to establish the following chronology of events with reasonable accuracy:

887 BC – Ethbaal (father of Jezebel) becomes king of Tyre (age 16)
880 BC – Omri (father of Ahab) becomes king of Israel
880 BC – Athaliah is born
874 BC – Ahab becomes king of Israel
874/3 BC – Ahab marries Jezebel (age 16?)
865 BC – Athaliah (age 15) marries Jehoram of Judah
864 BC – Athaliah gives birth to Ahaziah[20]

It is clear from these strongly attested dates that Athaliah couldn't have been Jezebel's child because she was born about six years before Jezebel married Ahab. Athaliah could technically have been a child of Ahab by

---

[20] H.J. Katzenstein, "Who Were the Parents of Athaliah?," *Israel Exploration Journal*, Vol. 5, No. 3 (1955), 194-197.

another wife, but that becomes more problematic because no other wives of Ahab are mentioned with royal claims for their children.

So Katzenstein concludes that Athaliah must have been the immediate daughter of Omri and therefore a very young sister of Ahab. When Omri died, she grew up as a young orphan in the court of Ahab ("daughter of Ahab") in order to represent his house in marriage to Judah. "She was educated under the supervision of Queen Jezebel and so influenced by that Tyrian princess. This makes plausible the character of Athaliah and her leanings to the Tyrian worship, which she witnessed daily in Samaria and later tried to introduce in Jerusalem."[21]

The Rechabites

One of the enigmatic groups of characters that arise in the story of Jezebel in 1 and 2 Kings is the Rechabites. There is very little about them in the Bible, but they end up playing a significant role in the end of the Omride rule over Israel and the establishment of Jehu's kingdom. So they make an appearance in the novel *Jezebel* within the context of another important background concept in the Old Testament: the Remnant.

We only read about the Rechabites at the end of 2 Kings 10 after Jehu has already killed Jezebel, Jehoram (Joram) of Israel, Ahaziah of Judah, and the seventy sons of Ahab. Then on the way to Samaria, Jehu runs into Jehonadab (or Jonadab) son of Rechab.

> 2 Kings 10:15–17:
> And when [Jehu] departed from there, he met Jehonadab the son of Rechab coming to meet him. And he greeted him and said to him, "Is your heart true to my heart as mine is to yours?" And Jehonadab answered, "It is." Jehu said, "If it is, give me your hand." So he gave him his hand. And Jehu took him up with him into the chariot. And he said, "Come with me, and see my zeal for the LORD." So he had him ride

---

[21] Katzenstein, "Who Were the Parents," 197.

in his chariot. And when he came to Samaria, he struck down all who remained to Ahab in Samaria, till he had wiped them out, according to the word of the LORD that he spoke to Elijah.

So Jehonadab has some apparent prior connection to Jehu because the new king speaks as if he already knew Jehonadab's heart. The ancient Jewish historian Josephus explains that Jehonadab was a "good and righteous man" who "had been his [Jehu's] friend of old."[22]

Jehonadab helped Jehu finish killing the surviving members of the house of Ahab. Later, Jehonadab went with Jehu to the temple of Baal to presumably take part in putting the priests of Baal to the sword (2 Kings 10:23-27). These two were warrior friends.

While there is no specific mention of Rechabites in 2 Kings, Jehonadab is referenced both times as "son of Rechab." The idea that Jehonadab had founded a community called the Rechabites actually comes from Jeremiah's prophecy that describes this community years after Jehu's story.

The word of the Lord comes to Jeremiah, telling him to "go to the house of the Rechabites and speak with them" (Jeremiah 35:2). Jeremiah orders the Rechabites to drink some wine, but the Rechabites refuse.

> Jeremiah 35:6–8:
> But they answered, "We will drink no wine, for Jonadab the son of Rechab, our father, commanded us, "You shall not drink wine, neither you nor your sons forever. You shall not build a house; you shall not sow seed; you shall not plant or have a vineyard; but you shall live in tents all your days, that you may live many days in the land where you sojourn." We have obeyed the voice of Jonadab the son of Rechab, our father, in all that he commanded us.

Yahweh uses the Rechabites as an example of faithfulness to vows as a rebuke against Israel's unfaithfulness. But notice that their vows were based

---

[22] Flavius Josephus, *Antiquities of the Jews* 9.132.

on Jonadab (alternate spelling of Jehonadab), son of Rechab. That's our man, the friend of Jehu.

Their peculiar vows of not drinking wine, and not living in built homes, or engaging in agriculture have been compared with holy Nazirite vows. Scholars have brought some historical interpretation to light that I incorporated into the novel *Jezebel*.

Herbert Huffman links the Rechabites to the tent-dwelling, metal-working Kenites descended from Tubal-Cain. He explains that their primitivist lifestyle was …

> … probably an attempt to reenact a notion of life patterned on the wilderness period, or a kind of counter-cultural reaction to the excesses of the prosperous, indulgent life in the Omride period in Israel…The wilderness period was a time without the comforts of established cities or fields and without sacrifices or oblations, and it was a time of special faithfulness… God will show Israel favor by letting them dwell in tents again as in the days of old… By renouncing a settled lifestyle, the Rechabites resemble the prophets, and they perhaps serve even as an intercessory group standing before God.[23]

Another oft-quoted commentator, Frick, explains, "The Hebrew name [Rechab] also can be the basis for the word "chariot." A guild of artisans would of necessity be somewhat nomadic in lifestyle, moving to ply their trade. The prohibition against wine becomes a possible caution against… the "loose lips sink ships" syndrome in this munitions craft, for chariots were certainly major elements in defense arsenals of the day."[24]

In his commentary on 2 Kings, T.R. Hobbs further adds, "that Jehonadab was associated with chariotry in some way, either as a rider or as a member of the chariot-making guild, is most attractive. It would explain Jehu's interest in gaining the support of such a man, especially if he had access to vehicles of

---

[23] Herbert B. Huffmon, "Rechab, Rechabites," ed. Katharine Doob Sakenfeld, *The New Interpreter's Dictionary of the Bible* (Nashville, TN: Abingdon Press, 2006–2009), 744.
[24] Gerald L. Keown, *Jeremiah 26–52, vol. 27, Word Biblical Commentary* (Dallas: Word, Incorporated, 1995), 196.

war. The question Jehu asks Jehonadab also echoes the establishment of military alliances."[25]

This became the foundation for my depiction of Jonadab and the Rechabites in *Jezebel* as the tent-dwelling chariot-makers as well as pure Yahwists in their religion who are protected by the archangels.

Within the context of a corrupt Israel full of idolatry, the Rechabites would be considered part of what the Scriptures call "the remnant." Remnant theology is rooted in the blessings and curses of Deuteronomy (Deuteronomy 4:25-27; 28:15-68), where Yahweh promised to destroy Israel and scatter her to the ends of the earth if she didn't obey Yahweh. And the only reason why Yahweh withheld his judgment for so long was for the sake of the remnant of true believers within the larger body of apostate Israel. God holds back punishment of the whole for the sake of the remnant of elect.

Isaiah wrote about the coming destruction and exile of apostate Israel and yet how a remnant would return to the land (Isaiah 6:11-13; 10:20-22) and that a remnant would also return from the Babylonian exile of Judah (Isaiah 46:3-4). Ezekiel too speaks of a remnant of God's spiritually chosen survivors (Ezekiel 6:7–9; 7:16; 14:22f.; 24:26). Isaiah predicts that another remnant would be saved when Messiah came (Isaiah 4:2-4; 11:11–16; 37:30–32). Micah echoes this return from exile (Micah 2:12; 4:6-8) at the incarnation of Jesus (Micah 5:2-5), as does Joel (Joel 2:32), Obadiah (Obadiah 17), and Zephaniah (Zephaniah 3:12). Jeremiah too writes of the remnant of a new heart and a new covenant (Jeremiah 23:3; 31:7-9, 31-34). And these are by no means an exhaustive list.

But the notion of the Remnant actually begins with the story of Elijah. The Apostle Paul explains Remnant theology from our very story of Elijah and Baalism. As in the Old Covenant, so in the New Covenant. The Jewish believers in Messiah in the first century were the true remnant of "God's people" in the midst of an apostate Israel that rejected Jesus and were ultimately judged.

---

[25] T. R. Hobbs, *2 Kings, vol. 13, Word Biblical Commentary* (Dallas: Word, Incorporated, 1985), 128–129.

Romans 11:2–6:

God has not rejected his people whom he foreknew. Do you not know what the Scripture says of Elijah, how he appeals to God against Israel? "Lord, they have killed your prophets, they have demolished your altars, and I alone am left, and they seek my life." But what is God's reply to him? "I have kept for myself seven thousand men who have not bowed the knee to Baal." So too at the present time there is a remnant, chosen by grace. But if it is by grace, it is no longer on the basis of works; otherwise grace would no longer be grace.

I carried this Remnant theology to its fruition in my novel series *Chronicles of the Apocalypse (paid link)*, which takes place in the time just after Paul wrote those words to the Romans. Christians were spared the destruction of Israel, Jerusalem, and the temple in AD 70 when they fled to the mountains in response to Jesus' warnings (Matthew 24:15-20). But it began with the story of Elijah and Yahweh's faithful followers as the true seed of Eve.

Chapter 2:
The Spiritual World of Israel

Monotheist or Polytheist?

The story of the novel *Jezebel: Harlot Queen of Israel* takes place in the middle of the ninth century B.C., a key turning point in biblical history. Because of Solomon's disobedience to Yahweh, the monarchy was split into two kingdoms, Israel in the north and Judah in the south, which launches the narrative that is 1 and 2 Kings, a forensic argument that confirmed Samuel the prophet's warning that Israel shouldn't have sought to have a king like the other nations. It reads like a heavenly Most Wanted list of spiritual criminals against God.

In my research for this novel, I was surprised at how inaccurate my view of ancient Israel had been in previous years.

Like most Christians raised in Sunday School, I had known of the apostasy both Israel and Judah experienced in worshipping other gods. But I had always seen it as a kind of reflection of our modern day world of Christianity. When I read that the Jews worshipped Baal, Asherah, Molech, or Astarte, I thought of it as a Christian whose addiction or besetting sin haunted them like some alcoholic or porn addict who give in to their "inner demons" and fall off the wagon, only to confess and repent and get back up again. So the Jews were spiritual addicts who would fall off the monotheist wagon and worship other gods, only to confess and repent and get back up again.

But this isn't really how it was. The biblical text and archaeology confirms that the Jews were not monotheists with occasional polytheist episodes. They were more like polytheists with occasional monotheist episodes. For the most part, the king dictated the direction of the people's religious observances. At the split of the monarchy, the king of the northern ten tribes, Jeroboam, made two golden calves just like the one in the wilderness, for which God destroyed thousands of Hebrews. He placed one of those idols in the city of Dan in the far north of his territory and the other in the city of Bethel in the far south. He also built pagan temples on high places and appointed priests from among the people who were not Levites as God had commanded (1 Kings 12:28-32). This action virtually established a blasphemous religion of idolatry to which the ten northern tribes of Israel ascribed. Those golden calves were not destroyed until the Assyrian exile in 722 B.C. (Dan) and Josiah's reform in 621 B.C. (Bethel: 2 Kings 23:15–16). Those calves stood with their idolatrous cult in Israel for two hundred years.

The calves most likely represented Yahweh, not Baal or some other deity, which is technically not polytheism. But the prophetic narrative of 1 and 2 Kings considers that idolatry to be so crucial to the judgment of the exile that "the sins of Jeroboam" and "way of Jeroboam" are phrases used repeatedly of subsequent kings who never destroyed those golden calves.[1] One after another with a few exceptions, they would walk "in the sins of Jeroboam" by continuing the high places and golden calf worship.

Solomon promoted actual polytheism when he created sacred "high places," altars and temples built on hills for Molech the underworld god of the Ammonites, Chemosh, chief god of the Moabites, and Astarte, the Queen of heaven and goddess of the Sidonians (1 Kings 11:5-8). The very son of David who built the temple of Yahweh in Jerusalem also built high place temples *for other deities*. Let that sink in. It's both astonishing and disturbing.

And these gods, along with Baal and others, were worshipped by the Jews for hundreds of years until the Assyrian and Babylonian exiles. The prophets blamed the exile precisely on this fact (2 Kings 17:6–12). If one charts the forty kings of the divided monarchy as listed in 1 and 2 Kings, it becomes readily apparent that the one unifying factor between almost every one of them is some form of false worship of God or gods, described euphemistically as "doing evil in the sight of the Lord"[2] or "walking in the sins of his father."[3]

There were some righteous kings in those several hundred years who did remove some idols. But even those only removed them for a short time and

---

[1] 1Kings 14:16; 15:30; 16:19, 26, 3; 22:52; 2Kings 3:3; 10:28; 13:2; 14:24; 15:9, 24, 28.

[2] 1King 14:22; 15:34; 16:19, 25; 2King 8:27; 13:2, 11; 14:24; 15:18, 28; 16:2; 17:17; 21:20; 23:32, 37; 24:9, 19.

[3] 1 King 15:3, 25; 2 King 8:18. 27; 16:2; 21:20.

never removed all of them—or the high places.[4] This means that for hundreds of years Israelites never failed to have some false gods they worshipped along with Yahweh. The good kings are sometimes described as mostly "doing right," *yet* not taking down the high places or the asherim idols.[5] The hero of the Jezebel story, Jehu, who wiped out Baal worship in Israel, nevertheless didn't take down the golden calves when he became king (2 Kings 10:28-29). Baal worship was brought to Judah by Jezebel's step-daughter Athaliah, thriving for another two hundred years.

The most well-known reformer was Josiah, who in 640 B.C. seemed to destroy every last vestige of idol worship in Judah like none before him. Unfortunately, even after him, new kings of Judah came in and restored those gods to the Jewish pantheon (2 Kings 23:31-24:19).

The Priesthood

The truth of the matter is that the ancient Jews of this time period were fundamentally polytheistic, not monotheistic. And it wasn't just the monarchy that was so. It was also the priesthood of the temple in Jerusalem. One would think that the priests of the very temple of God would promote monotheism. But according to Scripture, even they engaged in polytheistic cult rituals for most of the time that the temple was erect in Jerusalem. You read that correctly. The "holy" temple of Solomon was from its origin a temple used for idolatrous polytheism.

The author of 2 Kings tells us that the first great reformer, Hezekiah, removed the high places, broke the pillars, and cut down the asherah in the temple sometime around 716 B.C. But there was one other image in the temple that had been there from the beginning: the bronze serpent.

---

[4] 1 King 15:14; 22:43; 2King 13:6; 14:4; 15:4, 14, 35; 16:4;17:10-11; 21:3;

[5] 1King 15:11-14; 22:43; 2King 13:3-4; 15:3-4; 34-35.

2 Kings 18:4:
And [Hezekiah] broke in pieces the bronze serpent that
Moses had made, for until those days the people of Israel
had made offerings to it (it was called Nehushtan).

The bronze serpent had been made in the wilderness wandering by Yahweh's orders as a totem for healing. Israel had grumbled against God, so he sent fiery serpents among them as judgment. When they cried out in repentance, God had Moses cast the serpent as an image, and whoever looked upon it, would be healed (Numbers 21:4-9).[6]

But 2 Kings informs us that the Israelites had turned a temporary talisman of deliverance into an image of worship. We can't know for sure how long the Israelites made offerings to Nehushtan. Was it the two hundred-fifty years of the temple's existence, or was it the entire seven hundred years since the original event? In either case, it was hundreds of years of priest-led idolatry.

But the temple also had an idolatrous asherah pole in its walls for most of the three hundred and seventy years of its existence. Asherah poles, or *asherim*, will be explained later. But for now, they were carved wooden images that represented the goddess Asherah and bore her name. Scholar Raphael Patai explains this phenomenon:

> To sum up, we find that the worship of Asherah, which had been popular among the Hebrew tribes for three centuries, was introduced into the Jerusalem Temple by King Rehoboam, the son of Solomon, in or about 928 B.C.E. Her statue was worshiped in the Temple for 35 years, until King Asa removed it in 893 B.C.E. It was restored to the Temple by King Joash in 825 B.C.E. and remained there for a full century, until King Hezekiah removed it in 725 B.C.E. After an absence of 27 years, however, Asherah was back again in the Temple: This time it was King Manasseh who replaced her in 698 B.C.E. She remained in the Temple for 78 years, until the great reformer King Josiah removed her in 620

---

[6] Ironically, this bronze serpent on a pole idol has evolved into the caduceus, an icon of two serpents on a pole with angelic wings as a symbol for medical practice.

B.C.E. Upon Josiah's death eleven years later (609 B.C.E.), she was again brought back into the Temple, where she remained until its destruction 23 years later, in 586 B.C.E. Thus it appears that, of the 370 years during which the Solomonic Temple stood in Jerusalem, for no less than 236 years (or almost two-thirds of the time) the statue of Asherah was present in the Temple, and her worship was a part of the legitimate religion approved and led by the king, the court, and the priesthood and opposed by only a few prophetic voices crying out against it at relatively long intervals.[7]

We know that this pole was not merely a passive image sitting there in the temple complex because during the reforms of Josiah, 2 Kings states that Josiah took out sacred garments woven for the asherah in the temple as well as "vessels made for Baal, for Asherah, and for all the host of heaven" and burned them outside Jerusalem in the Kidron valley (2 Kings 23:4, 7). These sacred vessels in the temple were paraphernalia used in cultic practices of active polytheistic worship.

But I want to draw your attention to the fact that there were not merely cultic vessels for Asherah in the temple, but for Baal as well. This means that by the time of Josiah, Nehushtan, Asherah, and Baal had all been worshipped for years in the Jerusalem temple along with Yahweh.

Susan Ackerman goes so far as to say that "it was the norm in the southern kingdom in the ninth century, the eighth century, and the seventh century to worship both Yahweh and Asherah in the state temple in Jerusalem. The zeal of the reformer kings, Asa, Hezekiah, and Josiah, to remove the Asherah cult was the exception."[8]

It doesn't matter how much lip service one gives to Yahweh, if you have sacred images of an animal and a goddess along with cultic implements for three gods that you actively serve in your sole temple for decades, your priests are serving more than one god. It is fair to say that the Jewish priests were not monotheists with occasional polytheist episodes. Rather, they were polytheists

---

[7] Raphael Patai, *The Hebrew Goddess Third Enlarged Edition* (Detroit MI: Wayne State University Press, 1967, 1978, 1990), 50.

[8] Susan Ackerman, "The Queen Mother and the Cult in Ancient Israel," *Journal of Biblical Literature 112* (1993): 391.

with occasional monotheist episodes. It's easy to see why Yahweh grew so angry at them to the point of exiling them into the hands of their pagan lovers' gods. They were sharing Yahweh's house in Jerusalem with the goddess Asherah, as well as Baal, and Nehushtan.

The People

Much of the Old Testament was written by the educated scribal or royal class. So it tends to focus on the actions of rulers, judges, and kings. It doesn't really describe the life of common folk outside of those who make an important impact on the redemptive history of Israel. Archaeological finds in recent years have helped fill in the blanks of the common Jewish family in the Promised Land. And that common life was quite polytheistic indeed.

Archaeologist William Dever uncovers Israelite folk religion based on both the Bible and archaeological finds. He argues that the folk religion of the commoner "in the streets" was often very distinct from the religious cult of the ruling class in the palace or temple. This would make sense when you consider they didn't have mass communication. Uneducated farmers and shepherds out in the wilderness would carry on their folk religion with little distraction from directives by the priesthood miles away in Jerusalem.

I will address most of these elements in individual chapters as they arise. But here is Dever's brief summary list of the activities of Israelite folk religion:

> A list of proscribed activities would be long and complex, mostly derived from the Deuteronomistic and prophetic writings, but it could be summed up as follows.
> 1. Frequenting local shrines (bâmôt)
> 2. Setting up standing stones (massëbôt)
> 3. Making of images of various deities
> 4. Venerating the goddesses
> 5. Burning incense
> 6. Baking cakes for the "Queen of Heaven" [Astarte]
> 7. Making vows
> 8. "Weeping for Tammuz" [a Babylonian deity]

9. Performing rituals having to do with childbirth and children
10. Holding marzëah feasts [cult of the dead]
11. Conducting funerary rites; "feeding the dead"
12. Making pilgrimages to holy places and saints' festivals
13. Engaging in various aspects of astral and solar worship
14. Divining and "magic," except by priests
15. Sacrificing children (?)

All these things, mostly discussed above, are condemned by the male writers of the Hebrew Bible as "idolatrous," that is, non-Yahwistic. But their inclusion implies that the majority of people, not just an easily ignored minority, were doing them — and, I would argue, principally doing them in a family context where women played a highly significant role. I have also argued that all this was part of "Yahwism," at least until the 7th century B.C. attempts at reform.[9]

Dever is a critical scholar and an unbeliever. But he also avoids both extremes of Minimalism and Maximalism. Minimalism seeks only to cynically disprove the Bible with archaeology while Maximalism seeks only to naïvely prove the Bible with archaeology. Both extremes tend to be close-minded to counter-factual evidence. So despite his secular bias, Dever remains a respectable voice in biblical archaeology. And that archaeology has uncovered many examples of all these artifacts of folk religion in manifold locations throughout the land of ancient Israel.[10]

Here is where all the difference lies. Critical scholars. because of their presupposition of anti-supernaturalism (there is no supernatural), interpret these facts within an evolutionary framework constructed to conclude that the monotheist religion of Israel evolved out of polytheism. They refuse to allow the

---

[9] William G. Dever, *Did God Have a Wife?: Archaeology and Folk Religion in Ancient Israel* (Grand Rapids, MI: Eerdmans Publishing, 2005), 237.

[10] See William G. Dever, *The Lives of Ordinary People in Ancient Israel: Where Archaeology and the Bible Intersect* (Grand Rapids, MI; Cambridge, U.K.: William B. Eerdmans Publishing Company, 2012) and William G. Dever, *Did God Have a Wife?: Archaeology and Folk Religion in Ancient Israel* (Grand Rapids, MI: Eerdmans Publishing, 2005). Also, Ziony Zevit, *The Religions of Ancient Israel: A Synthesis of Parallactic Approaches* (London, Continuum, 2001).

possibility that there is a God who speaks and interacts in history with humanity. Therefore, they conclude before even looking at the evidence that monotheism was artificially thrust upon the people by priests and rulers, not God. In other words, monotheism evolved out of polytheism. After all, if there is no God who speaks into history, then all claims of him doing so are by definition lies of those in power used to manipulate the masses or the common man. Natural evolution, not supernatural revolution is their interpretive paradigm.

Furthermore, they think that uncovering ubiquitous polytheism in Israel somehow debunks the Bible. This is another function of prejudicial bias. As scholar Benjamin Sommer points out,

> It is important to emphasize that the biblical texts largely portray the Israelites as polytheists, because many modern scholars somehow assume that the biblical texts must have said that Israelites were monotheists. A depressingly large amount of scholarly writing on this subject consists of an attempt to debunk the Bible by demonstrating something the Bible itself asserts – indeed, something the Bible repeatedly emphasizes: that Israelites before the exile worshipped many gods.[11]

On the other hand, some Maximalists get freaked out because the picture of such deeply-rooted widespread polytheism in Israel doesn't fit the paradigm of Jewish monotheism they've been taught to accept. It makes them fear that the secularists and Minimalists may be right with their revisionary history and therefore their faith is in vain. So these believers deny or try to ignore the facts to protect their own bias and presuppositions.

But this fear is unnecessary. There is a third way of understanding between these two extremes. We can acknowledge the fact that during these centuries, Israelites claimed monotheism of a kind (some scholars call it more accurately, *monolatry*), but were practical polytheists in disobedience to Yahweh. Kings, priests, and common men were all infected by this evil at different levels. And of course, there were no doubt many individuals or pockets of people who were true to Yahweh. In the story of Elijah and Jezebel,

---

[11] Benjamin Sommer, *The Bodies of God and the World of Ancient Israel* (NY: Cambridge University Press, 2009), 149.

we are told that there were seven thousand who did not bow the knee to Baal (1 Kings 19:18).

Acknowledging mass apostasy in Israel for centuries is not the same as claiming monotheism evolved out of polytheism. It simply reinforces the doctrine of Original Sin. Because of the Fall in the Garden, human nature is bent toward evil, not good. So of course if there is a God who is there and is not silent, then he would have to be constantly pulling his chosen people away from their inherent nature toward polytheism. That's supernatural revolution, not natural evolution.

This also makes the prophets and their extreme language of condemnation of Israel and Judah that much more spiritually meaningful. It means that God really was so frustrated with the depth of apostasy in his own people that he had to choose individual spokesmen to Israel (prophets) in order to get his message to them. And that polytheism was so ingrained in the people's nature that they wouldn't get rid of it and because of it, would ultimately be carried away into exile. The promises of Messiah drawing the twelve tribes back under Yahweh are for a distant future. For now, the Jews lived, moved, and breathed in idolatrous polytheism.

That is the picture I tried to capture in my *Jezebel* novel, an accurate portrayal of the kind of religious world in which kings, priests, and commoners lived and worshipped.

The Watchers

I explained in the Note to the Reader at the beginning of *Jezebel* that I employ the Deuteronomy 32 worldview, or divine council motif, as a fantasy element to tell the supernatural side of the story of Jezebel and Elijah. The basic premise is that there is a spiritual world of principalities and powers whose stories are linked to earthly rulers.

Deuteronomy 32 tells the story of Israel and how she had come to be God's chosen nation. Moses begins by glorifying God and then telling them to "remember the days of old."

Deuteronomy 32:8–9:
When the Most High gave to the nations their inheritance,
> when he divided mankind,
he fixed the borders of the peoples
> according to the number of the sons of God.
But the Lord's portion is his people,
> Jacob his allotted heritage.

The context of this passage is the Tower of Babel incident in Genesis 11 when mankind was divided. Rebellious humanity sought divinity in unified rebellion, so God separated them by confusing their tongues, which divided them into the seventy nations (of Gentiles) described in Genesis 10 and their ownership of those bordered lands as the "inheritance" of those peoples.

But inheritance works in heaven as it is on earth. The people of Jacob (Israel) would become Yahweh's allotted inheritance while the other seventy Gentile nations were the allotted inheritance of the *Sons of God*.

So who were these Sons of God who ruled over the Gentile nations (Psalm 82:1-8)? Some believe they were human rulers. Others argue for their identities as supernatural principalities and powers. I am in the second camp. In my *Psalm 82* book, I prove why they can't be humans and must be heavenly creatures.

The phrase "Sons of God" is a technical term that means divine beings from God's heavenly throne court (Job 1:6; 38:7), and they are referred to with many different titles. They are sometimes called "heavenly host" (Isaiah 24:21-22[12]), sometimes called "holy ones" (Deuteronomy 33:2-3[13]), sometimes called "the divine council" (Psalm 82:1[14]), sometimes called "Watchers" (Daniel 4:13, 17, 23), and sometimes called "gods" or *elohim* in the Hebrew (Deuteronomy 32: 17, 43; Psalm 82:1; 58:1-2). Yes, you read that last one correctly. God's Word calls these beings *gods*.

But fear not. That isn't polytheism. The word "god" in this sense is a synonym for "heavenly being" or "divine being" whose realm is that of the spiritual. It doesn't mean uncreated beings who are all-powerful and all-

---

[12] See also Deut 4:19 with Deut 32:8-9; 1 King 22:19-23.

[13] See also Psalm 89:5-7; Heb 2:2.

[14] See also Psalm 89:5-7.

knowing. Yahweh alone is that God. Yahweh is the God of gods (Deuteronomy 10:17; Psalm 136:2). He created the other *elohim* ("gods"). These "gods" are created angelic beings who are most precisely referred to as Sons of God.

The narrative is this. Before the Flood, some of these heavenly Sons of God rebelled against Yahweh and left their divine dwelling to come to earth (Jude 6), where they violated Yahweh's holy separation and mated with human women (Genesis 6:1-4). This was not a racial separation, but a spiritual one. Their corrupt hybrid seed were called "nephilim" (giants), and their effect on humanity included such corruption and violence on the earth that Yahweh sent the Flood to wipe everyone out and start over again with Noah and his family.

Unfortunately, after the Flood humanity once again united in evil while building the Tower of Babel, a symbol of idolatrous worship of false gods. So Yahweh confused their tongues and divided them into the seventy nations. Since mankind wouldn't stop worshipping false gods, the living God gave them over to their lusts (Romans 1:24, 26, 28) and placed them under the authority of the fallen Sons of God whom they worshipped. Fallen spiritual rulers for fallen humanity (Psalm 82:1-7). It's as if God said to humanity, "Okay, if you refuse to stop worshipping false gods, then I will give you over to them and see how you like them ruling over you."

Deuteronomy 32 hints at a spiritual reality behind the false gods of the nations, calling them "demons" (Deuteronomy 32:17; also Psalm 106:37-38). The Apostle Paul later ascribes demonic reality to false gods as well (1 Corinthians 10:20; 8:4-6). The New Testament continues this ancient notion that spiritual principalities and powers lay behind earthly powers (Ephesians 6:12; 3:10). The two were inextricably linked in historic events. As Jesus indicated, whatever happened in heaven also happened on earth (Matthew 6:10). Earthly kingdoms in conflict are intimately connected to heavenly powers in conflict.[15]

When earthly rulers battle on earth, the Bible describes the host of heaven battling with them in spiritual unity. In Daniel 10, hostilities between Greece and Persia is accompanied by the battle of heavenly Watchers over those nations (described as spiritual "princes").

---

[15] Daniel 10:12-13, 20-21; 2Kings 6:17; Judges 5:19-20.

Daniel 10:13, 20-21:
The <u>prince of the kingdom of Persia</u> withstood me twenty-one days, but Michael, one of the <u>chief princes</u>, came to help me, for I was left there with the kings of Persia. ...Then he said, "Do you know why I have come to you? But now I will return to fight against the prince of Persia; and when I go out, behold, the <u>prince of Greece</u> will come. But I will tell you what is inscribed in the book of truth: there is none who contends by my side against these except <u>Michael, your prince</u>."

When Sisera fought with Israel, the earthly kings and heavenly authorities (stars or host of heaven) are described interchangeably in unity.[16]

Judges 5:19–20:
"The kings came, they fought; then fought the kings of Canaan...From heaven the stars fought, from their courses they fought against Sisera.

When God punishes earthly rulers, he punishes them along with the heavenly rulers ("host of heaven") above and behind them.

Isaiah 24:21–22:
On that day the LORD will <u>punish the host of heaven, in heaven, and the kings of the earth, on the earth</u>. They will be gathered together as prisoners in a pit; they will be shut up in a prison, and after many days they will be punished.[17]

This notion of territorial archons or spiritual rulers is biblical and carries over into intertestamental literature such as the Book of Enoch and others.[18] It

---

[16] See also 2 Kings 6:15-17 where Elisha's servant has his spiritual eyes opened to see the myriad of heavenly warriors surrounding Israel preparing to battle Syria.

[17] Interestingly, this passage of Isaiah is not clear about what judgment in history it is referring to. But the language earlier in the text is similar to the Flood when it says, "For the windows of heaven are opened, and the foundations of the earth tremble. 19 The earth is utterly broken, the earth is split apart, the earth is violently shaken. 20 The earth staggers like a drunken man; it sways like a hut; its transgression lies heavy upon it, and it falls, and will not rise again." So this may be another passage that uses a Flood reference tied in with the Watchers and their punishment.

[18] 1 En. 89:59, 62-63; 67; Jubilees 15:31-32; Targum Jonathan Deut. 32, Sect. LIII; 3Enoch 48C:9, DSS War Scroll 1Q33 Col. xvii:7, Targum Jonathan, Genesis 11, Section II.

is one of the foundational storylines of this series, Chronicles of the Watchers, as well as Chronicles of the Nephilim and Chronicles of the Apocalypse.

In the Bible, the term "Watchers" only appears in Daniel 4, where a Watcher, also called a "holy one," came down from heaven to proclaim to Daniel the "decree of the Watchers" that Nebuchadnezzar would go mad like a beast (Daniel 4:13-17, 23). Though the Watchers of Daniel 4 are not specifically equated with the "princes" over the kingdoms of the nations in Daniel 10, they are considered by ancient Jews to be synonyms. The Watchers over the nations were the princes or principalities of those nations.

Two examples of how the ancient Jews interpreted Deuteronomy 32:8-9 illustrate this notion of territorial principalities watching over nations.

> Jubilees 15:31-32:
> (There are) many nations and many people, and they all belong to him, but <u>over all of them</u> he caused <u>spirits to rule so that they might lead them astray from following him</u>. But over Israel he did not cause any <u>angel or spirit to rule</u> because he alone is their ruler and he will protect them.
>
> Targum Jonathan, Deuteronomy 32, Section LIII:
> When the Most High made allotment of the world unto the <u>nations</u> which proceeded from the sons of Noach [Noah], in the separation of the writings and languages of the children of men at the time of the division, He cast the lot among the <u>seventy angels, the princes of the nations</u> with whom is the revelation <u>to oversee the city</u>.[19]

But it is the book of 1 Enoch that uses the term "Watchers" most commonly of these territorial princes or angels or spirits or holy ones. The Sons of God of Genesis 6 are called Watchers all throughout 1 Enoch.[20] And

---

[19] See also 1 Enoch 89:59; 90:25, 3Enoch 48C:9, DSS War Scroll 1Q33 Col. xvii:7, Targum Jonathan, Genesis 11, Section II; Philo, On the Posterity of Cain and His Exile 25.89; Concerning Noah's Work as a Planter 14.59; On the Migration of Abraham 36.202; 1 Clement 29; Origen, First Principles 1.5.1. Thanks to Don Enevoldsen for some of these passages. Walter Wink footnotes a plenitude of texts about the 70 angel "gods" over the 70 nations in the Targums in Walter Wink. *Naming the Powers: The Language of Power in the New Testament* (The Powers : Volume One) (Kindle Locations 2235-2242). Kindle Edition.

[20] 1 Enoch 10:9, 15; 12:2-6; 13:10; 14:1-3; 15:9; 16:1-2.

those Sons of God are described in the Old Testament as Yahweh's heavenly host that surround him in his divine council.

Job describes the Sons of God as divine beings who were heavenly host present at the creation (Job 38:4-7) and who gathered around Yahweh, along with the satan, to council with him and perform his decrees (Job 1:6-7; 2:1-6). 1 Kings 22:19-23 depicts these same "host of heaven" as spirits surrounding Yahweh who do his bidding. Psalm 82 and 89 describes the assembly of heavenly host as his "divine council" of "gods," "holy ones," and "Sons of the Most High" (82:6), in other words, Sons of God.

All these terms are used synonymously for the divine beings of God's heavenly host, the Sons of God to whom Deuteronomy 32:8 declared were allotted the nations for an inheritance to watch over (territorial powers).

So the Bible says that there is demonic reality to false gods. But since those Sons of God who were territorial authorities over the nations were spiritually fallen Watchers, that makes them demonic or evil in essence. So what if they were the actual demonic beings behind the false gods of the ancient world? What if the fallen Sons of God were masquerading as the gods of the nations in order to keep humanity enslaved in idolatry to their authority? That would affirm the biblical stories of earthly events with heavenly events occurring in synchronization.

That is the biblical premise of the *Chronicles of the Watchers*. The pagan gods like Baal, Astarte, Asherah, and others, are actually fallen Sons of God, Watchers of the nations, crafting false identities and narratives as gods of the nations that are connected and reflected in the earthly events of human history and its rulers. For a detailed biblical defense of this interpretation see my booklet *Psalm 82: The Divine Council of the Gods, the Judgment of the Watchers and the Inheritance of the Nations.* (paid link)

1 Kings 22

My favorite Bible passage about the divine council is the story of King Ahab asking for the prophet Micaiah's advice on attacking Ramoth-gilead. I've included this story in the novel as an example of God's angelic heavenly host versus the fallen heavenly host who are the demonic gods of the nations.

The Spiritual World of Jezebel and Elijah

Micaiah describes a scenario so obviously supernatural that little explanation is required. Though the beings in the council here are not described as "gods" like elsewhere, they are described as the "host of heaven," which the Bible defines as divine beings or gods.[21]

> 1 Kings 22:19–23:
> And Micaiah said, "Therefore hear the word of the LORD: I saw the LORD sitting on his throne, and all the host of heaven standing beside him on his right hand and on his left; and the LORD said, 'Who will entice Ahab, that he may go up and fall at Ramoth-gilead?' And one said one thing, and another said another. Then a spirit came forward and stood before the LORD, saying, 'I will entice him.' And the LORD said to him, 'By what means?' And he said, 'I will go out, and will be a lying spirit in the mouth of all his prophets.' And he said, 'You are to entice him, and you shall succeed; go out and do so.' Now therefore behold, the LORD has put a lying spirit in the mouth of all these your prophets; the LORD has declared disaster for you."

The fascinating thing about this vision is that we get a glimpse into the actual process of counseling that God takes from his heavenly host. We see them surrounding his throne in counsel. We see them suggesting different things. Then God chooses one and empowers the spirit to accomplish his task. Most shocking of all, God is shown to be sovereignly ordaining "a lying spirit" to achieve his holy purpose of judgment. God ordains whatsoever comes to pass, though without himself being guilty of sin.

This may all seem rather scandalous to those Christians who prefer a simple and uncomplicated spiritual world where God sits on his throne and declares the end from the beginning without anyone's input. But biblical facts are the facts. God uses a bureaucracy of intermediary divine agents called gods, Sons of God, heavenly host, or holy ones, with whom he interacts and engages counsel.

Or as Psalm 82:1 puts it:

---

[21] Jeremiah19:13; Deut 4:19; 17:3; 29:26; 2 Chron 33:3-5; Acts 7:42-43.

God has taken his place in the divine council;
in the midst of the gods he holds judgment:

There are plenty of other passages that describe the divine council of heavenly beings around Yahweh who counsel with him and carry out his decisions with duly delegated legal responsibility. But this one shows it at work in our very story of Jezebel's husband Ahab.[22]

Leviathan

Leviathan is a crucial character in the Chronicles universe. It shows up in Chronicles of the Nephilim, Chronicles of the Apocalypse, as well as Chronicles of the Watchers. It is drawn from the ancient Near Eastern worldview that permeates the Bible.

Contrary to what some hyper-literalists may think, Leviathan is not a real world sea dinosaur or even an extinct sea monster. It is a spiritual image used by ancient Near Eastern religions to symbolize the chaos of the cosmos that their god fought to bring about his rule and order. The Babylonians called it Tiamat. The Canaanites called it Lotan, the Ugaritic translation for "Leviathan." Hebrews called it Leviathan and sometimes Rahab.[23]

The battle of divinity to create order out of chaos is called "chaoskampf" by theologians.[24] In Mesopotamian religion, Marduk fought and defeated Tiamat the sea dragon and split her in half to create the heavens and earth that

---

[22] Deut 32:43 LXX; Zech 2:13-3:7; Jer 23:18-22. And there are other passages where the divine council is not mentioned, but scholars explain that the plural grammar of the speech and activity imply the heavenly court motif of God addressing the council (Gen 1:26; 11:3, 4, 7; Isaiah6:8; 40:1; 41:21-23).

[23] Leviathan: Job 3:8; 41; Psalm 74:13-14; Psalm 104:26; Isa 27:1. Leviathan is said to dwell in the Abyss in Job 41:24 (LXX). "[Leviathan] regards the netherworld [Tartauros] of the deep [Abyss] like a prisoner. He regards the deep [Abyss] as a walk." Job 41:34, Tan, Randall, David A. deSilva, and Logos Bible Software. The Lexham Greek-English Interlinear Septuagint. Logos Bible Software, 2009.
For Rahab, see: Isaiah51:9; Job 9:13; 26:12-13; Ps 87:4; Psalm 89:9-10.

[24] For Chaoskampf in the Bible, see: Psalm 89:9-10; Isaiah 51:9-10; Job 26:12-13. Psalms 18, 29, 24, 29, 65, 74, 77, 89, 93, and 104. Also, Exodus 15, Job 9, 26, 38, and Isaiah 51:14-16; 2 Samuel 22.

symbolized the establishment of Babylonian world power.[25] The Canaanite Baal fought and defeated Sea (Yam), River (Nahar), and Leviathan (Lotan) in order to become the Most High ruler of the Canaanite pantheon.[26]

So, Yahweh is depicted as fighting and defeating Leviathan to establish his covenantal order with Israel at Sinai.

> Psalm 74:13–17:
> You divided the sea by your might;
> > you broke the heads of the sea monsters on the waters.
>
> You crushed the heads of Leviathan;
> > you gave him as food for the creatures of the wilderness.
>
> You split open springs and brooks;
> > you dried up ever-flowing streams.
>
> Yours is the day, yours also the night;
> > you have established the heavenly lights and the sun.
>
> You have fixed all the boundaries of the earth;
> > you have made summer and winter.

In the above psalm, the Red Sea deliverance of the Israelites ("dividing the sea") was the metaphor of God taking them out of the chaos of pagan Egypt. As in other ancient religions, Yahweh is depicted as defeating the sea, which also represented chaos to land dwellers. And Leviathan is in that sea as its instrument of power. But Yahweh crushes the heads of the sea dragon of chaos, and the creatures of the desert feast on his body. This banquet of eating the flesh of Leviathan symbolizes Yahweh's victory and is a common theme that appears in both biblical and extrabiblical Jewish poetry.[27]

The book of Revelation describes the victory of Christ over his enemies in chapter 19 as the "great supper of God" where the birds of prey eat the flesh of his defeated foes (19:17). While Leviathan is not included in this Revelation passage, it is the same kind of nature banquet motif as described in Psalm 74 with

---

[25] *Enuma Elish*, Tablet IV, lines 104-105, 137-138, 144.

[26] See KTU 1.3:3.38-41.

[27] For 2nd Temple examples of the feast of Leviathan and Behemoth, see 4Ezra 6:47-52; 2Apoc. Bar. 29:4; 1 Enoch 60: 7-9, 24.

creatures feasting on the flesh of the enemies of God. The banquet of flesh was a common way of symbolizing deliverance from and victory over one's enemies.

Leviathan does show up in Revelation as the seven-headed sea dragon who is the satanic enemy of chaos against God's people.[28] Once again, the sea dragon's defeat is symbolically linked to God establishing a new order, namely the new covenant kingdom of God in Christ's blood (Revelation 12:9-11).

But did the monster grow some new heads in this new incarnation? Not necessarily. If one looks closely at the fourteenth verse of Psalm 74 (especially in the Hebrew), it says that Leviathan has multiple *heads*, plural, not *head*, singular (Yahweh "crushed the *heads* of Leviathan"). And it is no coincidence that the Leviathan of the Canaanite Baal epic also has multiple heads (seven).[29]

But the last component of Psalm 74 above is the creation language that reminds the reader of Genesis 1. God separates day and night, establishes the heavenly host, and makes the seasons (v. 15-17). This is not some unconnected jump back to the creation of the universe. It is another cosmic metaphor of the covenant in terms of a "heaven and earth." Right after Yahweh delivers them through the sea, he brings them to Sinai, where he establishes his covenant order. The Mosaic covenant was a spiritual cosmos, a heaven and earth of God's operations with his people. Yahweh delivers his people, destroys the dragon of chaos with victory, and creates his covenantal order with Israel, a new "cosmos."

Hyper-literalist assumptions may cause distress in the believer who thinks this would mean that the Red Sea deliverance was "just a myth" or a spiritual symbol that didn't really happen in history. But this is simply a misunderstanding of the nature of ancient storytelling. Everything is not all "literal" or all "symbolic." It is very common for biblical writers to describe historic events with poetic or symbolic flair. So the Red Sea deliverance connected to the Sinai covenant was an historic event. But it also had spiritual ramifications so important they had to be described using symbolic terms of Leviathan and creation.

---

[28] See Rev 12:3-13:4; 16:13-16; 20:2-3.
[29] KTU 1.5:1:30

Leviathan can't be a literal physical creature because it is destroyed and eaten here in Psalm 74, yet is described by Isaiah as being alive then slain *in the future* at another victory of God, namely, the coming of Messiah (Isaiah 27:6, 9).

> Isaiah 27:1:
> In that day the LORD with his hard and great and strong sword will punish Leviathan the fleeing serpent, Leviathan the twisting serpent, and he will slay the dragon that is in the sea.

Leviathan is a spiritual symbol of the chaos that battles against order. But this *chaoskampf* in the Bible is not the same as pagan versions of it, where there is a dualist equivalence between the combatants, and either one might win. For example, Genesis 1 depicts Leviathan very differently for its theological purpose. We read of God's Spirit hovering over the dark "face of the deep" (v. 2), which is "without form and void," or "an unfilled wasteland" (Hebrew: *tohu wa-bohu*), an expression of that chaos which the sea tends to represent to the ancient world. The Hebrew word behind "deep" is *tehom*, which scholars argue is a linguistic connection to that sea dragon Tiamat. But in this context, there is no *chaoskampf* battle depicted. God simply speaks, and order is established through the separation of things.

When a sea dragon does appear, it is simply one of many sea creatures God created to swarm in the sea.

> Genesis 1:21:
> So God created the great sea creatures [*tannim*] and every living creature that moves, with which the waters swarm...
> And God saw that it was good.

The Hebrew word for "sea creatures" (*tannim*) is a word that is translated elsewhere as *dragon*.[30] Though Leviathan is not used here, the intent of the chapter is to demythologize the elements of the natural world that pagan cultures had divinized, including not only the sun, moon, and stars, but the sea (chaos) and the dragons that resided there.

---

[30] Isaiah 51:9. "Serpent, dragon, sea-monster" Francis Brown, Samuel Rolles Driver, and Charles Augustus Briggs, *Enhanced Brown-Driver-Briggs Hebrew and English Lexicon* (Oxford: Clarendon Press, 1977), 1072.

The imagery of *chaoskampf*, sea, and dragon are used poetically in some Bible passages to communicate the notion of God's creation of order out of chaos. In other passages, those mythopoeic symbols are tamed with ease and without a dualistic struggle because they are after all symbols in the service of their creator.[31] In the Bible, Leviathan has no chance of winning as he does in pagan mythology. All things are subject to the sovereign control of Yahweh, even chaos and evil.

One last element bears discussion related to Leviathan. In the novel *Jezebel: Harlot Queen of Israel*, Jezebel is portrayed as having a tattoo of Leviathan on her back. This connects her spiritually to both Leviathan *and* Asherah, a key figure in the story. Asherah was considered the mother of the gods in Canaanite mythology. She was the consort of the high god El, and as such was mother of Baal. Though Jezebel was a priestess of Astarte, there is some evidence that over time, Asherah, Astarte, and even Anat may have blended into one another as different names of one goddess.[32] One of the epithets of Asherah was "Lady of the Sea," or "Lady who Treads the Sea." Some scholars suggest that the epithet can be translated, "Lady who Treads the Sea Dragon."[33] The theological interconnections of all these images with the Asherah whom Israel embraced becomes readily apparent.

See my book *When Giants Were Upon the Earth (paid link)* for more on the theological meaning of Leviathan and its interaction with other fantastical motifs in the Bible.

---

[31] In Job 41, God's questions to Job about being able to make Leviathan a servant or "play with him as with a bird" are obvious implications that God does so with Leviathan as a domesticated pet. See also Psalm 104:26. See also "sea creatures" (tannim: dragons) Psalm 148:7; Psalm 74:13; Isaiah 51:9.

[32] William G. Dever, *Did God Have a Wife?: Archaeology and Folk Religion in Ancient Israel* (Grand Rapids, MI: Eerdmans Publishing, 2005), 220.

[33] John Day, "Asherah in the Hebrew Bible and Northwest Semitic Literature," *Journal of Biblical Literature* 105 (1986): 388.

Chapter 3:
The Gods of Canaan

Baal

In 1929, an archeological excavation at a mound in northern Syria called Ras Shamra unearthed the remains of a significant port city called Ugarit, whose developed culture reaches back as far as 3000 BC.[1] Among the important finds were literary tablets that opened the door to a deeper understanding of ancient Near Eastern culture and the Bible. Those tablets included Syro-Canaanite religious texts of pagan deities mentioned in the Old Testament. One of those deities was Baal (alternate spelling of Ba'al).

In the Bible, Baal is used both as the name of a specific deity[2] and as a generic term for multiple idols worshipped by apostate Israel.[3] It was also used in conjunction with city names and locations, such as Baal-Hermon and Baal-Zaphon, indicating manifestations of the one deity worshipped in a variety of different Canaanite situations.[4] Simply speaking, in Canaan, Baal was all over the place. He was the chief god of the land. One could say he was the spiritual prince of Canaan as the angel Michael was the prince of Israel who fought the spiritual princes of Persia and Greece (Daniel 10:13, 20-21).

Though the Semitic noun *baal* means lord or master, it was also used as the proper name of the Canaanite storm god.[5] In the Baal epic from Ugarit, El

---

[1] Avraham Negev, "Ugarit," *The Archaeological Encyclopedia of the Holy Land*, 3rd ed. (New York: Prentice Hall Press, 1996).

[2] Judges 6; 1 Kings 18; 2 Kings 10.

[3] Judges 2:13; 1 Samuel 12:10; Jeremiah 2:23.

[4] "Baal," *DDD*, 136.

[5] Karel van der Toorn, Bob Becking, and Pieter Willem van der Horst, *Dictionary of Deities and Demons in the Bible* (*DDD*), 2nd ext. rev. ed. (Grand Rapids: Eerdmans, 1999), 132.

was the supreme father of the gods who lived on a cosmic mountain. A divine council of gods called Sons of El surrounded him, vying for position and power. When the god Sea (Yam) is coronated by El and given a palace, Baal rises up and kills Sea, taking Sea's place as Most High over the other gods (excepting El). A temple is built and a feast celebrated. Mot (Death) then insults Baal, who goes down to the underworld, only to be defeated by Mot. Anat, Baal's violent sister, seeks Death and cuts him up into pieces, then brings Baal's body back up to earth, where he is brought back to life, only to fight Mot to a stalemate.[6] This return of the storm and vegetation god is a common mythical representation of the annual death of winter and new life of spring and autumn.[7]

The temporary loss of Baal to the underworld is also reflected in Jezebel's name, which in Canaanite means "Where is the Prince?" a liturgical call that Canaanites proclaimed every harvest. It is also reflected in Elijah's taunt to the prophets of Baal on Mount Carmel when he wonders if their god is absent because he is asleep in the earth (1 Kings 18:27).

The reader will notice that I have depicted this mythical narrative in the novel as a real journey where Anat rescues Baal from Mot in Sheol. And it is spiritually connected to Elijah's drought and the confrontation on Mount Carmel, thus affirming the biblical notion of the connection between earthly events and heavenly principalities. I consider it biblical appropriation and subversion of pagan mythology by the Hebrew metanarrative.

In the novel, I depict the Baal that Jezebel brings to Israel as Baal-Hadad, the storm god. This is contrary to a commonly argued interpretation that the god referred to in the Mount Carmel confrontation is Melqart. The argument for the latter is that Melqart was the patron god of Tyre, his name meaning literally, "king of the city." Melqart was a Phoenician appropriation of Herakles, the Greek divinized warrior. When Elijah mocked the prophets of Baal, he said, "Cry aloud, for he is a god. Either he is musing, or he is relieving himself, or he is on a journey, or perhaps he is asleep and must be awakened."

---

[6] N. Wyatt, *Religious Texts from Ugarit*, 2nd ed., The Biblical Seminar, vol. 53 (London: Sheffield Academic Press, 2002), 36-39.

[7] "Baal," *DDD*, 134.

The Spiritual World of Jezebel and Elijah

Herakles was known as a philosopher ("musing") and for having gone on a hero's journey into the underworld. There was also a ceremony of "awakening" the god from his winter sleep. The taunt of Elijah is considered an allusion to elements of musing, journey, and awakening.[8]

But biblical scholars John Day and Mark Smith explain that there are significant problems with this interpretation and argue convincingly that the Baal of Jezebel is Baal-Shamem (another name for Hadad; it gets confusing sometimes with all the multiple names for one being!).[9] Baal-Shamem means "lord of the heavens." This Shamem/Hadad was a storm god who was also associated with the Greek god Zeus. The most significant element of the Mount Carmel episode was that it was a contest of whose god was the storm god, lord of the heavens, a result of the drought called by Elijah. Melqart was not a storm god while Shamem/Hadad was.

Smith points out that an ancient inscription on Carmel identifies the god of Carmel as Zeus Heliopolis, the namesake of Shamem/Hadad, not Melqart.[10] Day argues that there are no royal names in Tyre that incorporate Melqart into their nomenclature, a common ancient practice. But there are many Tyrian names that incorporate Baal (a common reference to Shamem/Hadad) into their names, not the least of which is Jezebel and her father Ethbaal.[11]

Regarding the taunt of Elijah, Smith writes that the notion of a sleeping god being awakened is common to deities throughout the Near East, including Yahweh (Psalm 44:24; 78:65). As illustrated above, the Baal epic depicts Hadad/Shamem as being held in the underworld by Mot and being brought back to life out of the "sleep of death" by Anat. Jezebel's name is a translation of the liturgical phrase Tyrians would chant to raise Baal from that sleep to bring the rains.

In fact, according to the Baal epic, it is Hadad (Shamem) who is captured by Mot (Death) and imprisoned in the underworld as dead, which represents

---

[8] John Day, *Yahweh and the Gods and Goddesses of Canaan (The Library of Hebrew Bible/Old Testament Studies)* (Bloomsbury T&T Clark, 2002), 74.

[9] John Day, *Yahweh and the Gods and Goddesses of Canaan (The Library of Hebrew Bible/Old Testament Studies)* (Bloomsbury T&T Clark, 2002), 74-77; Mark Smith, *The Early History of God: Yahweh and the Other Deities in Ancient Israel*, 2nd Edition (Grand Rapids, MI: Eerdmans, 1990, 2002), 68-71.

[10] Smith, *The Early History of God*, 71.

[11] Day, *Yahweh and the Gods*, 75.

the seasonal deadness of the weather and crops in winter. The question "Where is the Prince?" is given in the text as a call to the return of harvest rains.

> Parched are the furrows of the grand fields,
> May Baal restore the furrows of the ploughed land.
> Where is Mightiest Baal?
> Where is the Prince, Lord of the Earth?
> (KTU 1.6:4:1-5)[12]

So Elijah's taunt is a sarcastic answer to the Baal prophets' liturgical calling for their Lord. But rather than just the mockery of being awakened from the dead, Elijah adds other options of musing, going to the toilet, or being on a journey (perhaps a reference to Anat's journey to find Baal in the underworld). The contest on Mount Carmel was ultimately about ending the death of drought and returning the rains of harvest season. It was a contest of storm gods. Baal (Shamem/Hadad) was a storm god, Melqart was not.

When the prophets of Baal "cut themselves after their custom with swords and lances until the blood gushed" (1 Kings 18:28), this was a liturgical mourning ritual to bring Baal-Hadad back from the underworld. The activity was sympathetic magic, replaying Anat's own activity in the Baal epic before freeing Baal to bring the rains.

> With a stone [Anat] scrapes her skin,
> Double-slits with a blade.
> She cuts cheeks and chin,
> Furrows the length of her arm.
> She plows her chest like a garden,
> Like a valley she furrows her back:
> "Baal is dead! What of the peoples?"
> (KTU 1.6:1:2-8)[13]

What appears upon a cursory reading of the biblical text to be a mockery of Baal and his prophets turns out to be a complex subversion of their entire Baal-Hadad narrative and mythology. Elijah's wit and wisdom made him the

---

[12] Mark S. Smith and Simon B. Parker, *Ugaritic Narrative Poetry*, vol. 9, Writings from the Ancient World (Atlanta, GA: Scholars Press, 1997), 158–159.

[13] Smith and Parker, *Ugaritic Narrative Poetry*, 151.

holy Oscar Wilde of the ancient world (for more on God's use of sarcasm in the Bible, see my book, *The Imagination of God* (paid link).

While Melqart was a patron god of Tyre, he was not the only one. Shamem/Hadad was not only the head of the Phoenician pantheon but also had a temple at Tyre along with Melqart and Astarte. Shamem's temple is most likely the oldest on the island.[14]

Day concludes,

> Since the Baal promoted by Jezebel was the same Baal who had been worshipped by the Canaanite population of Israel and syncretistic Israelites, it can readily be understood how he gained such a large following. This would not be the case with Melqart, the city god of Tyre, and, as MJ. Mulder has emphasized, Ahab would have committed political suicide had he attempted to promote such a foreign god.[15]

The Image of Baal

I depicted the Baal temple idol in the novel as a seated bronze humanoid dressed in his conical Egyptian ateph headdress with horns of deity. His arms were outstretched for sacrifice over a pit of fire. Though we don't have any actual temple images as artifactual examples, I have drawn from the writings of the ancients who described such images in relation to human sacrifice, another component of Canaanite/Phoenician religion. Though these are much later in time than the ninth century B.C., it's the closest we can get. Here are two of them.

> Greek author Kleitarchos (4th century B.C.):
> Kleitarchos says that, out of reverence for Kronos [Baal], the Phoenicians, and especially the Carthaginians... There stands in their midst a bronze statue of Kronos [Baal], its hands

---

[14] H. Jacob Katzenstein, *The History of Tyre*, 2nd ed. (Beer Sheva, Israel: Negev Press, 1997), 89. Quoted in Jennifer Lynn Greig-Berens, *Jezebel: Religious Antagonist in Israel*, Masters Thesis (Oral Roberts University, 2011), 8.

[15] Day, *Yahweh and the Gods*, 76.

extended over a bronze brazier, the flames of which engulf the child. When the flames fall upon the body, the limbs contract and the open mouth seems almost to be laughing, until the contracted (body) slips quietly into the brazier."[16]

Historian Diodorus Siculus (1st century B.C.):
There was in their city a bronze image of Cronus [Baal], extending its hands, palms up and sloping toward the ground, so that each of the children when placed thereon rolled down and fell into a sort of gaping pit filled with fire.[17]

The Temple of Baal

In the novel, Ahab builds the temple of Baal in Jezreel, the summer royal residence, rather than in Samaria, the royal capital of Israel. A common belief is that the Baal temple was built in the city of Samaria because 1 Kings 16:32 says Ahab "erected an altar for Baal in the house of Baal, which he built in Samaria."

But archaeologist Yigael Yadin has provided compelling evidence that the temple was actually built in the city of Jezreel rather than Samaria.[18] This is not to say the Bible is incorrect. The word "Samaria" is used in the text as both a reference to the city as well as the governmental state (1 Kings 13:32; 16:24; 2 Kings 21:1). The phrase in 1 Kings 16:32 doesn't stipulate the city or the region as the temple's location, so it could be either.

But tellingly, archaeological excavations haven't unearthed a temple in the city of Samaria. Writer Jennifer Greig-Berens concludes from the evidence:

Due to Ahab's loyalty to a central Yahwist cult in the capital of Israel, it is unlikely he would have built a temple to Baal in that place and arouse the opposition of those loyal to

---

[16] Paul G. Mosca, Child Sacrifice in Canaanite and Israelite Religion: A study in Mulk, PhD Thesis, (Cambridge, MA, Harvard University, 1975), 22.

[17] Diodorus Siculus, *The Library of History*, Book 20, 14:4-7, Loeb Classical Library, 1954, 153, quoted in Henry B. Smith, Jr., "Canaanite Child Sacrifice, Abortion, and the Bible," *The Journal of Ministry and Theology*, 98.

[18] Yigael Yadin, "The 'House of Ba'al' of Ahab and Jezebel in Samaria, and that of Athalia in Judah," in *Archaeology in the Levant*, eds. Peter Roger Stuart Moorey and Peter Parr (Warminster, UK: Aris & Phillips, 1978).

monotheism in Israel. It may have been in Jezreel that Ahab set up a palace and temple in order for his new wife and her entourage to practice their Baal worship. Jezreel seems to be the center of Baalism in the biblical narratives and is in closer proximity to Mount Carmel, where the altar of Yahweh had been "torn down" and replaced with an altar to Baal (1 Kings 18:30). This is also the abode of Jezebel after the death of her husband and during the reign of her son, Joram.

Furthermore, the area of Jezreel is the usual focal point of prophetic fulfillment throughout the narratives: the location of Naboth's ancestral property (1 Kings 21:1-4); the place where the dogs would devour Jezebel (1 Kings 21:23); the place where Joram is assassinated (2 Kings 9:21-26); as well as where the heads of Ahab's "seventy sons" are sent and piled up next to the gate of the city during Jehu's revolt (2 Kings 10:8-9). By all accounts, Jezreel appears to be the central hub of Jezebel's proliferation of the Baal cult in Israel.[19]

I've drawn my description of the temple of Baal from archaeology. The most popular Phoenician designs known from Ugarit, Byblos, and other sites commonly include a long tripartite rectangular building, a pillared entrance with steps, and a long hall with an elevated holy of holies at the back where the image of the deity resided.[20]

This explains why the Baal temples are the same design as the Yahweh temple in Jerusalem. King Hiram of Tyre was hired by Solomon to help build Yahweh's house with Phoenician craftsmanship (1 Chronicles 14:1).[21]

Some Bible readers may fear this reeks of syncretism, melding foreign pagan religions with biblical religion. It's not syncretism but subversion. Subversion is defined as the appropriation and repurposing of a foreign cultural element into one's own cultural meaning. I've argued extensively in

---

[19] Jennifer Lynn Greig-Berens, *Jezebel: Religious Antagonist in Israel*, Masters Thesis (Oral Roberts University, 2011), 45-46.

[20] John H Walton, *Zondervan Illustrated Bible Backgrounds Commentary (Old Testament): 1 & 2 Kings, 1 & 2 Chronicles, Ezra, Nehemiah, Esther*, vol. 3 (Grand Rapids, MI: Zondervan, 2009), 71.

[21] See also 2 Chron 2:3, 7, 13-14.

my books *The Imagination of God* and *God Against the gods* (paid links) that God and his scriptural authors in both Old and New Testaments engage in extensive subversion of pagan imagination. The temple is but one example.

In ancient Near Eastern religion, the temple was considered the center of the cosmos. Its architecture and design was a microcosm that reflected the macrocosm of the universe. The temple was described as being situated on a "cosmic mountain," a holy hill where creation first began, along with a river that flowed out of the mountain as the source of eternal life.[22] So too in the Bible, God's temple was a designed microcosm of the universe (Psalm 78:68-69) on the holy hill, the cosmic Mount Zion (Psalm 43:3-4; Is 2), where an Edenic river of eternal life is symbolically described as flowing out of its gates (Ezekiel 47:1-12).

But whereas similarities help to illuminate similar meaning, differences change meaning and make all the difference in the world. Differences are where subversion rather than syncretism takes place. Whereas the image of the deity was housed in the holy of holies of pagan temples, there was no image of Yahweh in his temple because of his prohibition of images. But also, he wanted to make it clear that the temple was only a sacramental symbol of connection between heaven and earth. "Heaven is my throne, and the earth is my footstool; what is the house that you would build for me, and what is the place of my rest?" (Isaiah 66:1-2).

Yahweh Versus Baal

This subversion of pagan imagination was not only in archaeological artifacts but also in literary poetry and prose. What critical scholars interpret as syncretistic evolution of Canaanite religious ideas are actually polemical subversions of those ideas by biblical authors.

It has long been known that the Old Testament contains many allusions and reflections of Canaanite literature. Some of those similarities include language used by Canaanites of Baal that were also used by the Hebrews of

---

[22] John H. Walton, *Ancient Near Eastern Thought and the Old Testament: Introducing the Conceptual World of the Hebrew Bible* (Grand Rapids: Baker, 2006), 113-34.

Yahweh. A side-by-side sampling of Ugaritic texts with Scripture illustrates strong echoes of Canaanite imagery in the biblical storytelling (see below).

UGARITIC TEXTS[23]	OLD TESTAMENT
Baal sits… in the midst of his divine mountain, Saphon, in the midst of the mountain of victory. Seven lightning-flashes, eight bundles of thunder, a tree-of-lightning in his right hand. His head is magnificent, His brow is dew-drenched. his feet are eloquent in wrath. (KTU 1.101:1–6)[24] The season of his rains may Baal indeed appoint, the season of his storm-chariot. And the sound of his voice from the clouds, his hurling to the earth of lightning-flashes (KTU 1.4:5.5–9) At his holy voice the earth quaked; at the issue of his lips the mountains were afraid. The ancient mountains were afraid; the hills of the earth tottered. (KTU 1.4:7.30–35) now your foe, Baal, now your foe the Sea you must smite; now you must destroy your adversary! Take your everlasting kingdom, your eternal dominion! (KTU 1.2:4.9–10) Then Baal returned to his house [temple]. 'Will either king or commoner establish for himself dominion in the earth? (KTU 1.4:7.30–35)	"Yahweh came from Sinai… At His right hand there was flashing lightning… There is none like the God of Jeshurun, Who rides the heavens to your help, And through the clouds in His majesty… And He drove out the enemy from before you, And said, 'Destroy!' So Israel dwells in security, The fountain of Jacob secluded, In a land of grain and new wine; His heavens also drop down dew." (Deuteronomy. 33:2, 26–28) The voice of the LORD is over the waters; the God of glory thunders, the LORD, over many waters… The voice of the LORD breaks the cedars; the LORD breaks the cedars of Lebanon… The voice of the LORD flashes forth flames of fire [lightning]. The voice of the LORD shakes the wilderness… And in His temple everything says, "Glory!" Yahweh sits enthroned over the flood; Yahweh is enthroned as King forever. (Psalm 29:3–11)

---

[23] The abbreviation *KTU* stands for "Keilalphabetische Texte aus Ugarit", the standard collection of this material from Ugarit.

[24] All these Ugaritic texts can be found in N. Wyatt, *Religious Texts from Ugarit*, 2nd ed., The Biblical Seminar, vol. 53 (London: Sheffield Academic Press, 2002).

Critical scholars interpret these similarities as syncretistic evolution—i.e., that the Jews originally worshipped Baal and transformed him into Yahweh. But this ignores the more germane explanation of similarities as being a common usage of images in polemical arguments. Remember, the differences make all the difference in the world. And those differences in meaning are loud and clear. Yahweh inspires his authors to use water and storm language to reflect God's polemic against the so-called storm god Baal.

Comparing the texts yields identical words, memes, and metaphors that suggest God is engaging in polemics against Baal through scriptural imagery and storytelling. It isn't Baal who rides his cloud chariot from his divine mountain Saphon but Yahweh who rides the clouds from his divine Mount Sinai (and later, Mount Zion). It isn't Baal who hurls lightning flashes in wrath but Yahweh whose lightning flashes destroy his enemies. It isn't Baal whose dew-drenched brow waters the land of Canaan but Yahweh who drops dew from heaven to Canaan. It isn't Baal's voice that thunders and conquers the waters, resulting in his everlasting temple enthronement, but Yahweh whose voice thunders and conquers the waters, resulting in his everlasting temple enthronement.

Psalm 29 (quoted in part above) is so replete with poetry in common with Canaanite poetry that many Ancient Near East scholars have concluded it is a Canaanite hymn to Baal rewritten with the name Baal replaced by the name Yahweh.[25] God was not only *physically* dispossessing Canaan of its inhabitants but *literarily* dispossessing the Canaanite gods as well. Old Testament appropriation of Canaanite culture is a case of subversion, not syncretism — overthrowing cultural narratives as opposed to blending with them. See my book [God Against the gods (paid link)](#) for an in-depth examination of this biblical literary use of creative subversion.

Asherah

Another major deity who has an important role to play in the story of Jezebel's ninth century Israel is Asherah (Athirat in Canaanite). This goddess has a

---

[25] Aloysius Fitzgerald, "A Note on Psalm 29," *Bulletin of the American Schools of Oriental Research*, no. 215 (October 1974), 62. A more conservative interpretation claims a common Semitic poetic discourse.

veiled yet significant presence in the Bible during this time period. In some ways, she may have had a more insidious effect on the Israelites than Baal ever had.

Scholar Raphael Patai introduces the Asherah of Canaanite mythology as a fertility goddess and the wife of El, the chief god.

> Her full name was "Lady Asherah of the Sea"—apparently, her domain proper was the sea, just as that of her husband El was heaven. She was, however, also referred to simply as Elath or Goddess. She was the "Progenitress [Mother] of the Gods": all other gods, numbering seventy, were her children, including Baal, Anath [Anat], Mot, and the other chief protagonists of the Ugaritic pantheon… Asherah's relationship to her husband El was not unlike that of an Oriental queen to her master: when entering into his presence, she would prostrate herself, whereupon El would kindly inquire after her desire. When Baal wished to obtain permission from El to build a house, he sent his mother Asherah to intercede with El. Upon the death of Baal, El asked Asherah to name one of her sons to succeed him as king. Asherah was a motherly goddess and as such she, together with her daughter Anath, served as the wet-nurse of the gods.[26]

Canaanite writings speak of a shrine of Asherah in Tyre, "the goddess of the Sidonians."[27] Archaeologist William Dever adds that excavated imagery of Asherah often involve her wearing an Egyptian-style Hathor wig and standing on the back of a lion or escorted by two lions, thus giving the great Mother Goddess the additional epithet, "The Lion Lady."[28]

---

[26] Raphael Patai, *The Hebrew Goddess 3rd Enlarged Edition* (Detroit, MI: Wayne State University Press, 1967, 1978, 1990), 37.

[27] N. Wyatt, "Asherah," ed. Karel van der Toorn, Bob Becking, and Pieter W. van der Horst, *Dictionary of Deities and Demons in the Bible* (Leiden; Boston; Köln; Grand Rapids, MI; Cambridge: Brill; Eerdmans, 1999), 99.

[28] William G. Dever, *Did God Have a Wife?: Archaeology and Folk Religion in Ancient Israel* (Grand Rapids, MI: Eerdmans Publishing, 2005), 219-220.

Patai examines the manifold ancient artifacts found all over Palestine of clay figurines of nude women with protruding breasts and explains how they conform to stereotypical representations of Asherah. He concludes that Asherah was very popular with the common folk women of Israel, probably because she promoted fertility and facilitated childbirth.[29]

Dever imagines an ancient cultural context of men spending "too much time with their noses stuck in the Torah" and the moral dilemmas of public life while being oblivious to their families' needs. Meanwhile, the women guided the family exercise of religious rituals and cult to safeguard their loved ones and therefore regarded themselves as morally superior to the men.[30] Depending on your presuppositions, one could see this as an anachronistic projection of modernity back upon the ancient world or as a reflection of the unchanging nature of gender weaknesses.

But Karel van der Toorn agrees that in the Bible Israelite women are often portrayed as displaying a greater religious sensibility than their husbands:

> All in all, then, ancient Israelite religion played a double role in the lives of women. While legitimating their subservient social position, it opened the possibility as well of an intense religious experience. In this way, it gave a compensation on one level for what it had taken on another. As it seems, Israelite women eagerly seized upon this possibility.[31]

As a goddess of fertility, Asherah was a predictable point of connective identity for Israelite women. Asherah appears in the Bible dozens of times. But the word (singular: *asherah*; plural: *asherim*) is used for both the goddess and the image used to represent the goddess.[32] Asherah was often depicted in Canaanite art as a tree of life.[33] The Septuagint (Greek translation of the Old

---

[29] Patai, *The Hebrew Goddess*, 39.

[30] Dever, *Did God Have a Wife?*, 250.

[31] Karel Van Der Toorn, "Female Prostitution in Payment of Vows in Ancient Israel," *Journal of Biblical Literature* 108 (1989): 195.

[32] Raphael Patai, *The Hebrew Goddess 3rd Enlarged Edition* (Detroit, MI: Wayne State University Press, 1967, 1978, 1990), 38.

[33] The most famous of these references is the Ta'anach cult stand that depicts Asherah as both a naked mistress of animals and a tree of life. See Dever, *Did God Have a Wife*, 219-220.

Testament) translated the word "asherim" as "sacred groves," and the high places with asherim were often referred to as "every high hill and green tree" (1 Kings 14:23). Because of these connections with trees, Dever concludes, "Thus it seems clear that originally in ancient Israel there was a goddess named Asherah, who was associated with living trees and hilltop forest sanctuaries, and who could sometimes be symbolized by a wooden pole or an image of a tree."[34]

Though it isn't clear exactly what these asherim poles looked like, a perusal of the Old Testament passages gives the reader some clues. They are wooden (Judges 6:26), probably tree-like in symbolism (Deuteronomy 16:21), that were "made" (2 Kings 21:3), "carved" (2 King 21:7), could be "chopped down" (Deuteronomy 7:5), "cut down" (2 Kings 18:4), and "burned with fire" (1 King 15:13). They were often "planted" beside altars of Baal (Deuteronomy 16:21; Judges 6:28) or altars of Yahweh (2 Kings 23:6) and often spoken of together with Baal (Judges 3:7). Whatever they looked like, they represented the presence of the mother goddess, most likely as a consort to both Baal and Yahweh.

In more recent years, discoveries of inscriptions at Kuntillet ʿAjrûd in the Sinai and Khirbet El-Qom near Lachish have supported the idea that it was common for Israelites to consider Asherah as a wife or consort of Yahweh. Though interpretations are varied, some scholars argue the inscriptions may be translated as in the following examples:

- I bless you before Yahweh of Samaria and his Asherah.
- Yahweh of Teman and his Asherah.
- Blessed by Uriyahu by Yahweh.
- By his Asherah, he has saved him.[35]

They all reflect the common localization of a deity with a city (Yahweh of Samaria), but there is disagreement over whether Asherah refers to the distinct deity or to the images that represent her. In either case, there is an intimate pairing of Yahweh with the goddess Asherah.

---

[34] William G. Dever, *Did God Have a Wife?: Archaeology and Folk Religion in Ancient Israel* (Grand Rapids, MI: Eerdmans Publishing, 2005), 102.

[35] Othmar Keel, Chirstoph Uehlinger, *Gods, Goddesses, and Images of God in Ancient Israel* (Minneapolis: MN, Fortress Press, 1998), 229-239. Ziony Zevit translates the phrases without the possessive, "his," thus indicating "Yahweh and Asherah," still as consorting deities. Ziony Zevit, *The Religions of Ancient Israel: A Synthesis of Parallactic Approaches* (London, Continuum, 2001), 361, 373.

I've already examined the fact that there was an asherah in the Jerusalem temple for most of its existence (236 out of 370 years). As indicated in the texts, asherim were usually "planted beside altars" (Deuteronomy 16:21; Judges 6:28), so the asherah in Jerusalem was most likely beside the stone altar in the inner court of Yahweh's temple. All the evidence seems to affirm that the norm of the official Judahite religion included Asherah as Yahweh's consort. The reformers such as Hezekiah and Josiah were the anomaly (righteous though they were). When Josiah eliminated the asherah and other idolatrous elements of worship from the temple in the seventh century, he included rooms for male cult prostitutes "where the women wove garments for the asherah" (2 Kings 23:7). These were apparently garments that were used to clothe the asherah in some ritualistic manner.[36]

Strangely, Asherah was not always treated with the same level of condemnation as was Baal in the Scriptures. In our particular story of Jezebel, Elijah calls upon Ahab to send his 450 prophets of Baal and Jezebel's 400 prophets of Asherah to Mount Carmel (1 Kings 18:19). But in the showdown, only the prophets of Baal are ever mentioned as being there and as being slaughtered. Either the prophets of Asherah didn't show up and were spared, or they *did* show up and were spared. Either way, they don't appear to have been killed along with the Baal prophets. If they had been, the writer of Kings would have certainly exulted in it. After executing Jezebel, Jehu is described as "wiping out Baal" from Israel, and "demolishing" his temple. But no word is written of Asherah. As already noted above, the priesthood of Jerusalem had kept an asherah in Solomon's temple for 236 out of its 370 years, two-thirds of its existence. It seems that worship of the goddess had a more entrenched grip on Israelites and Jews than did Baal or other deities.

Who says there wasn't female privilege in the ancient patriarchy?

Critical scholars interpret all this polytheistic polyamory as evidence that Asherah worship was a normal part of Israel's religion, claiming Asherah as Yahweh's wife, and that only later "fundamentalist" priests got rid of the other gods for the sake of their own religious bias. Confessional scholars agree with

---

[36] "The word here rendered "garments" is Hebrew bāttîm, which surely cannot have its usual meaning "houses" but rather, as originally suggested by A. Šanda, is probably cognate with Arabic batt "woven garment." John Day, "Asherah in the Hebrew Bible and Northwest Semitic Literature," *Journal of Biblical Literature 105* (1986): 406–407.

Yahweh and the prophets that it only showed God's wife Israel was committing spiritual adultery for most of their spiritual marriage, thus deserving exile (Jeremiah 3:1-9).[37]

My interpretation then of asherim in the novel as large poles with stylized tree branches of gold on the top and carved Asherah stories on the bottom is based on these hints of ancient totemic imagery. And my depiction of the Watcher known as Asherah reflects her influence on Israelites as a fertility goddess and "Mother of the gods," despite her subordination to Baal.

Astarte

Two other goddesses who show up in the novel of Jezebel are Astarte and Anat. They are depicted as being in competition for Baal's favor. Astarte is sent to Jerusalem because of their worship of her, while Anat is Baal's sister who journeys into Sheol to try to rescue him from Mot's death grip. These elements are all present in the Bible and in Canaanite lore. I've integrated them into the novel's storyline, giving them new meaning in a biblical context.

In Canaan, Astarte ("Ashtart" in Phoenician) was a goddess of fertility and war as well as a consort of Baal.[38] She had an astral identification with the planet Venus, thus earning her the epithet "Astarte of the Highest Heavens," and "Queen of Heaven,"[39] linking her to the Mesopotamian goddess Ishtar. Jezebel's father Ethbaal was originally a high priest of Astarte from Sidon who became king of Tyre.[40]

---

[37] See also: Hosea 2:2; Jeremiah 3:6; Exodus 34:15–16; Leviticus 17:7; Numbers 15:39; 25:1; Deuteronomy 31:16; Judges 2:17; 8:27, 33; 1 Chronicles 5:25; 2 Chronicles 21:11, 13; Psalm 106:39; Isaiah 1:21; Jeremiah 2:20; 3:1–9; 5:7; Ezekiel 6:9; 16:15–17, 20, 22, 25–36, 41; 23:5–8, 11, 14, 19–19, 27–30, 35, 44; 43:7, 9; Hosea 1:2, 2:2, 4–5; 3:3; 4:10–15, 18; 5:3–4; 6:10; 9:1; Joel 3:3; Amos 7:17; Micah 1:7; Nahum 3:4.

[38] N. Wyatt, "Astarte," ed. Karel van der Toorn, Bob Becking, and Pieter W. van der Horst, *Dictionary of Deities and Demons in the Bible* (Leiden; Boston; Köln; Grand Rapids, MI; Cambridge: Brill; Eerdmans, 1999), 110.

[39] John Day, *Yahweh and the Gods and Goddesses of Canaan (The Library of Hebrew Bible/Old Testament Studies)* (Bloomsbury T&T Clark, 2002), 149. Susan Ackerman, "At Home with the Goddess," in *Symbiosis, Symbolism, and the Power of the Past: Canaan, Ancient Israel, and Their Neighbors from the Late Bronze Age through Roman Palaestina*, ed. William G. Dever and Seymour Gitin (Winona Lake, IN: Eisenbrauns, 2003), 461.

[40] Josephus, *Antiquities of the Jews* 8.13.2.

In the Bible, Astarte is referred to in Hebrew as Ashtaroth or Ashtoreth, goddess "of the Sidonians" (1 Kings 11:5; 1 Samuel 12:10). Like Jezebel's name in the text, Ashtoreth is most likely a deliberate mockery of her name by using the vowels of the Hebrew word for shame, *bosheth*, with the consonants of Astarte.[41] The word "shame" was already used explicitly to refer to Baal in Jeremiah 11:13 and Hosea 9:10.

> Jeremiah 11:13:
> For your gods have become as many as your cities, O Judah, and as many as the streets of Jerusalem are the altars you have set up to shame, altars to make offerings to Baal.

Though the prophets and Deuteronomist authors of Kings may have had contempt for the goddess, the Hebrew populace at large surely did not. The Israelites had worshipped her along with Baal since the days of the judges hundreds of years earlier (Judges 2:13).[42] While she is absent in the text during the reign of David (1 Samuel 12:10-11), Astarte seems to have returned with a particularly strong hold on Judah when Solomon built high places for her in Jerusalem (1 Kings 11:5, 33).

Astarte appears to be the "Queen of Heaven" that Jeremiah condemns with much rigor in Judah long after Israel is gone into the Assyrian exile (Jeremiah 44:15-23). The rituals of Astarte worship described by Jeremiah involve the whole household, but are apparently led by the wives, who are depicted as making offerings to the Queen of Heaven proudly without their husband's approval (44:19) and to whom they attribute their food and prosperity (v.17-18).

As biblical scholar Susan Ackerman conveys, Jeremiah reveals that the whole family was involved in the goddess worship, which included pouring libations, burning incense, and baking cakes.

> The *children* gather wood, the *fathers* kindle fire, and the
> *women* knead dough to make cakes for the Queen of Heaven

---

[41] John Day, *Yahweh and the Gods and Goddesses of Canaan (The Library of Hebrew Bible/Old Testament Studies)* (Bloomsbury T&T Clark, 2002), 214.

[42] See also Judges 10:6; 1 Sam 7:3-4; 12:10.

(Jeremiah 7:18). Still, despite this depiction of the whole family's involvement, I think that it is fair to say that the women's contribution—the actual making of the offering cakes—is the most religiously significant, and thus it is reasonable to see these women as somehow *especially* involved in the goddess's worship. Indeed, in the polemic against the Queen of Heaven cult in Jeremiah 44, Jeremiah seems to make exactly this point, since it is *women* who are specifically identified in Jeremiah 44:19 as those who have "burned incense to the Queen of Heaven and poured out libations to her... and made for her cakes in her image," and it is thus *women*, in the culmination of Jeremiah's fulminations (44:25), who are singled out for the prophet's special scorn.[43]

Perhaps Dever's claim of female-led folk religion is not so anachronistic after all.

Anat

Another goddess who plays significantly into the plot of the novel *Jezebel* is Anat. In the Ugaritic texts, Anat is a fertility goddess, the sister of Baal as well as his consort. *The Dictionary of Deities and Demons* (*DDD*) describes her as a "volatile, independent, adolescent warrior and hunter." Her epithet, Virgin Anat, is more a commentary on her age than her actual sexual status since she is considered sexually active with Baal. One passage in the Baal epic most likely describes her in the form of a heifer having sex with Baal eighty-eight times.[44] But her ability to remain active in the male realms of war and hunting is due to her failure to "grow up" to be a marriageable female.[45]

---

[43] Susan Ackerman, "At Home with the Goddess," in Symbiosis, Symbolism, and the Power of the Past: Canaan, Ancient Israel, and Their Neighbors from the Late Bronze Age through Roman Palaestina, ed. William G. Dever and Seymour Gitin (Winona Lake, IN: Eisenbrauns, 2003), 464.

[44] KTU 1.5.20; 1.10.

[45] P. L. Day, "Anat," ed. Karel van der Toorn, Bob Becking, and Pieter W. van der Horst, Dictionary of Deities and Demons in the Bible (Leiden; Boston; Köln; Grand Rapids, MI; Cambridge: Brill; Eerdmans, 1999), 37–38.

Susan Ackerman describes Anat's lust for violence from the pages of the Baal epic:

> The goddess adorns herself with a necklace of skulls and a girdle of hands (CTA 3.2.11-13). Her joy in battle is vividly described in this passage (CTA 3.2.23-28):
>
> She fought hard and looked,
> Anat battled and saw:
> Her liver swelled with laughter,
> Her heart was filled with joy,
> The liver of Anat was exultant,
> As she plunged knee-deep in the blood of the mighty,
> Up to her hips in the gore of warriors.
>
> Anat's violent and ruthless behavior is further evident in the epic of Aqhat, where she schemes against Aqhat and eventually kills him in order to gain possession of his magnificent bow and arrows (CTA 17.6; 18.4).[46]

In the novel, Anat with her special bow of Aqhat in hand seeks Baal in the underworld. According to the Baal epic, when she finds him...

> ...She grabs Mot by the hem of his garment,
> She seizes him by the edge of his cloak.
> She raises her voice and cries:
> "You, O Mot, give up my brother."
> And Divine Mot answers:
> "What do you desire, [Virgin] Anat?...[47]
> She seizes Divine Mot,
> With a sword she splits him,
> With a sieve she winnows him.
> With a fire she burns him,
> With millstones she grinds him,

---

[46] Susan Ackerman, *Under Every Green Tree: Popular Religion in Sixth-Century Judah*, (Atlanta: GA, Scholars Press, 1992), 51.

[47] KTU 1.6:2:6-9.

In a field she sows him.
The birds eat his flesh,
Fowl devour his parts,
Flesh to flesh cries out.[48]

Baal returns to the earth above, is seated on his royal throne once again, and the father god El rejoices…

…For Mightiest Baal lives,
The Prince, Lord of the Earth is alive.[49]

Anat was not to be trifled with. And her pride is displayed not merely in her defeat of Mot but in her claim to have defeated Leviathan (Lotan) and Sea (Yam), "a conquest elsewhere attributed to Baal and a necessary step towards Baal's acquisition of kingship."[50] As the saying goes, behind every successful god there stands a supportive goddess—or in this case, a usurping one.

The depiction in the novel of Sheol, through which Anat travels to find Mot's city, is based upon the Jewish cosmic geography mostly found in 1 Enoch. For details of that picture of the underworld, see below Chapter 4: Cosmic Geography, Sheol.

Though Anat is not referenced directly in the Old Testament, she is most likely alluded to in some passages relevant to her character as a patron of warriors.

The place-name of the city Beth-Anat (House of Anat) in the Bible indicates the presence of a temple of Anat in the city.[51] 1 Samuel 31:10 describes the Philistines as placing the slain King Saul's armor in "the temple of Ashtaroth" in Beth Shan. Recent discoveries of a temple of Anat in Beth

---

[48] KTU 1.6:2:30-37. Smith and Parker, *Ugaritic Narrative Poetry*, 155-156.

[49] KTU 1.6:3:20-21. Smith and Parker, *Ugaritic Narrative Poetry*, 158.

[50] For Baal's defeat of Leviathan, see: (KTU 1.2 iv; 1.5 i:1–3) P. L. Day, "Anat," ed. Karel van der Toorn, Bob Becking, and Pieter W. van der Horst, *Dictionary of Deities and Demons in the Bible* (Leiden; Boston; Köln; Grand Rapids, MI; Cambridge: Brill; Eerdmans, 1999), 37–38.

[51] "Beth-Anat (bet-'andt) in Naphtali (Josh. 19.38; Judg. 1.33); Beth-Anot (bet-'anot) in Judah (Josh. 15.59), and Anathoth in Benjamin ('anatdt, in Josh. 21.18; 1 Kings 2.26 and "'natotin 1 Kings 2.26; Isa. 10.30; Jer. 1.1,11.21, 23, 32.7, 8, 9; 1 Chron. 6.45; Ezra 2.23; Neh. 7.27; cf. also the adjective 'the Anathothite', ha'annetoti in 2 Sam. 23.27, 1 Chron. 12.3 and Jer. 29.27; and hd'annetdtim 1 Chron. 11.28, 27.12)." John Day, *Yahweh and the Gods and Goddesses of Canaan (The Library of Hebrew Bible/Old Testament Studies)* (Bloomsbury T&T Clark, 2002), 132-133.

Shan, coupled with the possibility of the term "Ashtaroth" being used as a generic Akkadian language reference to a goddess without dignifying her name, point to a strong possibility that this was the temple of Anat. As the *DDD* writes, "Given Anat's clear portrayal as a warrior and a patron or guardian of warriors and royalty in extrabiblical sources, and given that we know she had a temple in Beth Shan, it makes good sense to suggest that the armor of a vanquished warrior-king would be brought to her temple by the grateful victors."[52]

The other biblical allusion to Anat can be found in the name of Shamgar ben Anat, a warrior who had killed six hundred Philistines with an ox goad (Judges 3:31; 5:6). Keep in mind that names in the ancient world and the biblical text often reflected character, origins, or destinies. The word "ben" means "son of." But since patronyms refer to male lineage, not females such as Anat, it is better seen as a metaphorical reference. Day argues it is most likely an honorific military title for a warrior, Shamgar, as a son of the goddess Anat, a not uncommon title in Canaan.[53] Is it a coincidence this mighty warrior of mass slaughter carries the name of a mighty deity of mass slaughter?

In the Ugaritic texts, Anat is a consort of Baal as is Astarte, thus placing them somewhat at odds, as portrayed in the novel. Though Astarte is more prominent in the Old Testament than her competitor Anat.[54]

Mot

Mot ("Death") is considered the supreme god of the underworld in Canaanite mythology. The Bible draws on imagery and language that echoes that narrative and subverts it into the biblical worldview, a subversion that the novel *Jezebel: Harlot Queen of Israel* continues in like manner.

The story of Mot and Baal in the Baal epic shows Mot addressing Baal, the one who "killed Litan [Leviathan], the fleeing serpent, the twisting serpent

---

[52] P. L. Day, "Anat," ed. Karel van der Toorn, Bob Becking, and Pieter W. van der Horst, *Dictionary of Deities and Demons in the Bible* (Leiden; Boston; Köln; Grand Rapids, MI; Cambridge: Brill; Eerdmans, 1999), 42.

[53] Day, *Yahweh and the Gods*, 134.

[54] Day, *Yahweh and the Gods*, 131.

with seven heads."[55] Mot does this as a way of building up Baal in order to show Mot's greater power when he captures him.

> Surely [Baal] will descend into Divine Mot's throat,
> Into the gullet of El's Beloved, the Hero. [56]

Mot's (Death's) boundless appetite is described as a gaping jaw that swallows his victims into the underworld. His mouth is:

> One lip to Earth, one lip to Heaven,
> a tongue to the Stars.[57]

In the novel, Baal is captured by being swallowed up into "Mot's jaws" in the Hinnom Valley outside Jerusalem, which leads down to Sheol.

In the Ugaritic literature, Baal is brought to Mot's underworld city, translated alternatively the Swamp, the Pit, his royal house, Filth, or the land of his inheritance.[58]

Hearing that Baal is dead, Anat journeys into the underworld to hunt down Mot. When she finds him, as described earlier, she cuts him into pieces, winnows him, burns him, grinds him, and sows him in the field for the birds to eat his flesh.[59] Baal returns to life on the earth above and is seated once again on his royal throne.[60] Later, Mot returns to argue with Baal and fight him, but he eventually acknowledges the storm god's rule on his throne.[61]

Sheol was the Hebrew word for the underworld of the dead.[62] I will discuss the geography of Sheol as a location in Chapter 4 on Cosmic

---

[55] KTU 1.5:1:1-4.

[56] KTU 1.5:1:4-8. Mark S. Smith and Simon B. Parker, *Ugaritic Narrative Poetry*, vol. 9, Writings from the Ancient World (Atlanta, GA: Scholars Press, 1997), 141.

[57] KTU 1.5:2:2-6. Smith and Parker, *Ugaritic Narrative Poetry*, 143. See also N. Wyatt, *Religious Texts from Ugarit*, 2nd ed., Biblical Seminar, 53 (London; New York: Sheffield Academic Press, 2002), 120.

[58] KTU 1.5:2:13-16. Coogan, Michael D.; Mark S. Smith. *Stories from Ancient Canaan, Second Edition* (Kindle Locations 5072-5073). Westminster John Knox Press. Kindle Edition.

[59] KTU 1.6:2:30-37.

[60] KTU 1.6:3:20-21.

[61] KTU 1.6:5:5-6:38.

[62] "Sheol," *DDD*, p 768.

Geography. For now, I will focus on the biblical use of the term as a metaphor for death and as an analogy of the Canaanite Mot.

The Old Testament uses personified descriptions of Sheol that are very similar to those of Mot. But the Hebrew writers don't treat Sheol as a personal god like Mot. In this way, the biblical text demythologizes and subverts the pagan god of death into a demonic phenomenon with real spiritual impact.

The Canaanite language of Death's (Sheol's) ravishing appetite and wide throat swallowing up life shows up in Old Testament texts:

> Isaiah 5:14:
> Therefore Sheol has <u>enlarged its appetite and opened its mouth beyond measure</u>, and the nobility of Jerusalem and her multitude will go down...
>
> Habakkuk 2:5 (NASB95):
> [The haughty man] <u>enlarges his appetite like Sheol</u>, And he is like death, <u>never satisfied</u>. He also gathers to himself all nations And <u>collects to himself all peoples</u>.
>
> Proverbs 1:12:
> Like Sheol let us <u>swallow them alive</u>,
> and whole, like those who go down to the pit.

Bible scholar John Day writes about these parallels of Sheol and Mot.

> Sheol is also referred to as swallowing people up in Proverbs 1.12, and its insatiable appetite is alluded to in Proverbs 27.20 and 30.15b-16. In Psalm. 49.15 (ET 14) death is a shepherd and those who go to Sheol are like sheep, "Like sheep they are appointed for Sheol; Death shall be their shepherd..." Although this is only poetic language, it recalls what is said of the god Mot in the Baal text, KTU 1.6.II.21-23, "I myself came upon the victor Baal, I myself made him as lamb in my mouth; he himself like a kid in my jaws was carried away." The same word "mouth" (pi) is used of Sheol in Psalm 141.7.

It seems clear that the Hebrews used the same kind of terminology for Sheol that Canaanites used of Mot. But in some cases, they go out of their way to seemingly subvert the pagan deity like this passage in Isaiah's "little apocalypse."

> Isaiah 25:8:
> He will swallow up death [Mot] forever; and the Lord GOD will wipe away tears from all faces, and the reproach of his people he will take away from all the earth.

As Day points out, in this case, Isaiah is positing an ironic power of Yahweh over Death (Mot). Whereas it is usually Death or Mot who does the swallowing, in this case it is the swallower that is to be swallowed up.[63] There are no gods who compare to Yahweh, the creator and sustainer of all things, Death included.

In Isaiah 28, the phrase "covenant with death" is used of Jerusalem's intermixing with foreign peoples and their gods (v. 11; 27:9). Spiritual apostasy is likened to a covenant with Mot.

> Isaiah 28:15:
> Because you have said, "We have made a covenant with death [Mot], and with Sheol we have an agreement, when the overwhelming whip [scourge] passes through it will not come to us, for we have made lies our refuge, and in falsehood we have taken shelter."

The first thing to notice in this passage is that covenants were only made with persons, usually a tribe or nation with a ruler or god. Making a covenant with Mot was not merely a metaphorical covenant with death as an abstraction. The covenantal language represented the spiritual unfaithfulness that Judah displayed toward Yahweh in going after other gods. Isaiah was saying that they thought they were covenanting with the gods Baal, Asherah, Astarte, Molech, and Chemosh, but they were actually covenanting with the god Mot, which represented their spiritual Death.

---

[63] Day, *Yahweh and the Gods*, 186.

God's judgment is described as a strong wind like a scourge upon them. As scholar Mark Smith argues, "Biblical descriptions of the east wind as an instrument of divine destruction may have derived from the imagery of Mot in Canaanite tradition...The juxtaposition of the east wind and personified Death in Hosea 13:14-15 may presuppose the mythological background of Mot as manifest in the sirocco."[64]

Speaking of Hosea 13, let's look closer at that passage. It addresses more than one deity in its reference.

> Hosea 13:14-15 (NRSV):
> Shall I ransom them from the power of Sheol?
> Shall I redeem them from Death [*Mot*]?
> O Death [*Mot*], where are your plagues [*Deber*]?
> O Sheol, where is your destruction [*Qeteb*]?
> Compassion is hidden from my eyes...
> the east wind shall come, a blast from the LORD,
> rising from the wilderness; and his fountain shall dry up,
> his spring shall be parched.
> It shall strip his treasury of every precious thing.

Death here is a strong allusion to the Canaanite Mot because of the reference to the east wind and the other two Hebrew words used of Death's power: "plagues" (*deber*) and "destruction" (*qeteb*). These two words are considered literary references to two Canaanite underworld deities as demons.[65]

In the Ugaritic Baal epic, the plague god Qeteb appears to be a kinsman of Mot. In the four places *qeteb* occurs in the Old Testament (Deuteronomy 32:24; Psalm 91:5-6; Hosea 13:14; Isaiah 28:2), it is translated in English as "pestilence" or "destruction," and is paralleled with Mot, Deber, or Resheph

---

[64] Mark Smith, *The Early History of God: Yahweh and the Other Deities in Ancient Israel*, 2nd Edition (Grand Rapids, MI: Eerdmans, 1990, 2002), 88.

[65] "The eschatological hymn in Hab 3 presents Deber and Resheph marching at Yahweh's side as His helpers. This follows the ancient Mesopotamian tradition according to which 'plague' and 'pestilence' are present in the entourage of the great god Marduk... On the other hand, in Ps 91:6 it is Yahweh who liberates his faithful from the fear of this nocturnal demon Deber, in parallel this time with Qeteb, another awesome destructive demon." del Olmo G. Lete, "Deber," ed. Karel van der Toorn, Bob Becking, and Pieter W. van der Horst, *Dictionary of Deities and Demons in the Bible* (Leiden; Boston; Köln; Grand Rapids, MI; Cambridge: Brill; Eerdmans, 1999), 232.

(another Canaanite underworld deity of plague[66]). The *DDD* concludes, "Qeṭeb is more than a literary figure, living as a spiritual and highly dangerous reality in the minds of poets and readers."[67] Deber "seems to be used a number of times in a personified sense as a demon or evil deity (Hab 3:5; Ps 91:3, 6; cf. Hos 13:14),"[68] and Resheph "is a demonized version of an ancient Canaanite god, now submitted to Yahweh."[69]

In the Bible, Qeteb (*destruction*), Deber (*plague*), Resheph (*pestilence*), and Mot (*death*) are all demonic realities.

Molech

Molech is a Canaanite god of the underworld. Though he only appears briefly in *Jezebel: Harlot Queen of Israel*, he is certainly significant in the big picture of the spiritual world of Judah at this time, as well as a prominent player in the storyline of my other series *Chronicles of the Nephilim*.

Until 1935, all scholars believed that the name Molech in the Old Testament referred to a god. Then new views came out of the academic community that the Hebrew word translated "Molech" or "Moloch," (*mlk*) was a kind of sacrifice rather than the name of a divinity. They argued that it was linguistically influenced by the Phoenician term *molk*, found in many sacrificial inscriptions in the Mediterranean world.[70]

But this problem has been put to rest in a way that reveals just who this Molech really is. John Day provides the answers in his excellent primer, *Yahweh and the Gods and Goddesses of Canaan*. Leviticus 20:5 declares Israel as

---

[66] *KTU* 1.82:3. "[Resheph] appears as a cosmic force, whose powers are great and terrible: he is particularly conceived of as bringing epidemics and death. The Hebrew Bible shows different levels of demythologization: sometimes it describes Resheph as a personalized figure, more or less faded, sometimes the name is used as a pure metaphor. At any rate it is possible to perceive aspects of the personality of an ancient chthonic god, whichs fits the image of Resheph found in the other Semitic cultures."
van der Toorn, Becking van der Horst, *DDD*, 703-704.

[67] N. Wyatt, "Qeteb," ed. Karel van der Toorn, Bob Becking, and Pieter W. van der Horst, *DDD*, 674.

[68] del Olmo G. Lete, "Deber," ed. Karel van der Toorn, Bob Becking, and Pieter W. van der Horst, *DDD*, 231–232.

[69] P. Xella, "Resheph," ed. Karel van der Toorn, Bob Becking, and Pieter W. van der Horst, *DDD*, 703.

[70] John Day, *Yahweh and the Gods and Goddesses of Canaan* (The Library of Hebrew Bible/Old Testament Studies) (Bloomsbury T&T Clark, 2002), 209

"whoring after Molech." This phrase of "whoring after" a god is used throughout the Bible in reference to many different deities of Canaan.[71] It is never used of people "whoring after a sacrifice." And all the verbs employed in connection with the Molech cult, "offering to," "giving to," "burning as an offering to," are actions toward a divine being, not toward a cultic ritual itself.[72]

The Old Testament is clear that Molech is a Canaanite deity, not a Phoenician one. His cult is described as a Canaanite abomination (Leviticus 18:21; 20:2-5). The Hebrew word for king is "melek," which uses the same consonants as Molech, so there is some kingly context inherent in the divine name. But as with the names Jezebel, Ashtoreth, and others, it is possible that the scribes of the later Hebrew text used the vowels of the Hebrew word for "shame" (*bosheth*) and inserted them in the consonants of Molech's name.

Day explains the external evidence for Molech as an underworld deity in Canaan:

> That there was such a deity [Molech] is shown by two Ugaritic serpent charms which mention him (KTU2 1.100.41 [Ugaritica V.I, RS 24.244] and KTU2 1.107.17 [Ugaritica V.8, RS 24.251]). In both places it is associated with the place name Ashtaroth in Transjordan, a place elsewhere connected in the Ugaritic texts with rp'u [Rephaim] (KTU2 1.108.1-2), indicating an underworld association. He also appears as Malik in various god lists and in personal names from Ebla, Mari, and Ugarit. Significantly, Malik is twice equated with Nergal, the Mesopotamian underworld god, once in an Old Babylonian god-list where we read Ma-lik = Nergal, and again in a later god-list from Ashur, which likewise has Ma-lik = Nergal. This clearly indicates an underworld deity.

In the Bible, Molech is connected with the underworld in key ways. First, Isaiah 57 describes child sacrifices "in the valleys, under the clefts of the rocks" (57:5), the activity most connected to the Molech cult. The text

---

[71] Exod. 34.15, 16; Lev. 17.7; Deut. 31.16; Judg. 2.17, 8.33.
[72] Day, *Yahweh and the Gods*, 210.

The Spiritual World of Jezebel and Elijah

describes the journey to that abominable altar as an adulterer seeking the bed of a foreign god.

> Isaiah 57:9:
> You journeyed to the king (*melek*) with oil and multiplied your perfumes; you sent your envoys far off, and sent down even to Sheol.

In this case, "king" (*mlk*) is most likely a double entendre of Molech (*mlk*). But notice that the king resides in Sheol, the underworld. And that underworld was connected to the valley location of Molech's cult in Jerusalem.[73]

The Molech cult was known for its child sacrifice, or "passing one's children through the fire" (2 Kings 23:10). The altar of this sacrifice was called a Tophet or Topheth, a place of burning, which once again used the vowels of "shame" (*bosheth*) inserted into the consonants of the Aramaic word for "burning place" (*tepat*).[74] We will discuss the details of human sacrifice later in Chapter 5. But this shameful and atrocious activity was infamously popular in the Valley of Hinnom just outside the southwest walls of Jerusalem. Yahweh condemned this infernal location through the prophet Jeremiah for their "high places of Tophets" where they "burned their sons and daughters in the fire" (Jeremiah 7:31). He then proclaimed the name of the valley would be changed from "Valley of the Sons of Hinnom" to "Valley of Slaughter" (7:32), a term that would come to refer to Gehenna or hellfire in later years of Second Temple Judaism. Molech was an underworld god of fire sacrifice of children. This is why I portrayed him in my novels as mole-like with a maze of underground tunnels beneath the Hinnom Valley of the Tophet outside Jerusalem.

In chapter 4, we'll look more closely at that underworld and the rest of the cosmic geography that fills the pages of Scripture and the novel of *Jezebel*.

---

[73] Day, *Yahweh and the Gods*, 215.

[74] J. F. Prewitt, "Topheth," ed. Geoffrey W. Bromiley, *The International Standard Bible Encyclopedia*, Revised (Wm. B. Eerdmans, 1979–1988), 876.

The Archangels

One of the ongoing series of characters that appear in all the Chronicles series of novels is the archangels. In the *Jezebel* novel, they are depicted as they are in previous stories as protecting God's people, most specifically the Remnant. Mikael (Michael) in particular is tasked with the protection of the bloodline of Messiah in Judah as he is considered the "prince of Israel," or the principality of the Hebrew nation, in the same way that gods like Baal are considered the principalities of the pagan nations. This is rooted in a biblical tradition.

The only archangels named explicitly in the Bible are Michael and Gabriel. Gabriel is well known in the New Testament as the angel who comes to herald the births of both John the Baptist (Luke 1:11-20) and Jesus the Messiah (Luke 1:26-35).

The angel Gabriel is described as "one having the appearance of a man" who explains visions to Daniel the prophet in Daniel 8:16 and 9:21. Though it isn't explicitly stated, some scholars believe Gabriel is also the unidentified angelic man who explains Daniel's vision of the spiritual principalities of the nations in Daniel 10.

In that vision, we hear about Michael, who is described as "one of the chief princes" (Daniel 10:13) and the spiritual prince of Daniel's people Judah (10:21; 12:1), who fights with Gabriel against the spiritual "princes" (principalities) of Persia and Greece.

> Daniel 10:12–13:
> Then [Gabriel] said to me... I have come because of your words. [13] The prince of the kingdom of Persia withstood me twenty-one days, but Michael, one of the chief princes, came to help me, for I was left there with the [human] kings of Persia.

> Daniel 10:20–21:
> Then he said... "But now I will return to fight against the prince of Persia; and when I go out, behold, the prince of Greece will come....there is none who contends by my side against these except Michael, your prince.

Daniel 12:1:

> "At that time shall arise <u>Michael, the great prince who has charge of your people</u>. And there shall be a time of trouble, such as never has been since there was a nation till that time. But at that time <u>your people shall be delivered</u>.

The underlying Hebrew word for "prince" (*sar*) in these passages can be used of human as well as spiritual rulers. But most scholars acknowledge that the context of these passages dictates a spiritual principality over earthly powers. As Bible scholar John Collins explains,

> The title "prince" does not necessarily imply less than divine status. The "prince of the host" in Daniel 8:11 is apparently the God of Israel. A precedent for the title "prince" being applied to an angel can be found in the [commander of the army of Yahweh] who appears in Josh 5:14. The title is used for the chief angelic powers at Qumran, for example, the "prince of lights" (1QS 3:20; CD 5:18) and the "prince of the dominion of wickedness" (1QM 17:5–6).[75]

This vision reveals the Deuteronomy 32 worldview played out in the unseen realm. The earthly kingdom of Persia was in battle with earthly Babylon, who held Judah captive, and so the spiritual prince of Persia was at war with the spiritual princes Michael and Gabriel, who were protecting Judah. When earthly Greece would come after Persia, their spiritual principalities too would fight in connection with the earthly battles of history (Deuteronomy 32:8-10; Judges 5:19-20; Isaiah 24:21-22; Ecclesiastes 17:17; Jubilees 15:31–32).[76]

The concept of *archangel* is drawn from the reference to Michael as one of the "chief princes" (Daniel 10:13). He is also called an archangel in Jude 9, and he is described in the Daniel passages above as the prince in charge of Israel who protects and delivers her (12:1).

---

[75] John Joseph Collins and Adela Yarbro Collins, *Daniel: A Commentary on the Book of Daniel*, ed. Frank Moore Cross, Hermeneia—a Critical and Historical Commentary on the Bible (Minneapolis, MN: Fortress Press, 1993), 375.

[76] Daniel L. Smith-Christopher, "The Book of Daniel," in *New Interpreter's Bible*, ed. Leander E. Keck, vol. 7 (Nashville: Abingdon Press, 1994–2004), 137.

There are two other places where Michael is described in his archangel capacity or leading the heavenly host. The first is in Jude, where a strange event is referenced that has no evidence in the Old Testament. Michael was said to have disputed with the devil over the body of Moses.

> Jude 9:
> But when the archangel Michael, contending with the devil, was disputing about the body of Moses, he did not presume to pronounce a blasphemous judgment, but said, "The Lord rebuke you."

The context of this passage is that Jude is talking about the false teachers of his time who "defile the flesh, reject authority, and blaspheme the glorious ones" (v. 8). This raises all kind of questions. If this story was not in the Old Testament, where did Jude get it? What did it mean to "dispute about the body of Moses"? And who are the glorious ones?

The story, though not available to us in any known manuscripts, was claimed by various early church fathers to have been taken from a book they had access to called by some *The Assumption of Moses* and by others *The Testament of Moses*. In either case, we no longer have the text. But it certainly opens the door to understanding how New Testament writers used Second Temple Jewish texts as sources in their canonical writing.

I try to make some sense out of the strange disputation over Moses's body in my novel [Caleb Vigilant (paid link)](). I believe it might have something to do with the fact that Moses's body had been transformed in some way by being in the presence of God. He was "shining," not unlike those heavenly host around God's throne (Exodus 34:29). Perhaps, the more time Moses spent in God's presence, the more his physical body transformed to be more like those Sons of God around the throne.

So, the "glorious ones" in Jude 8 are contextually the shining angels from God's throne. They are referred to earlier in the text when Jude writes of the angels who left their heavenly habitations in primeval days. "Blaspheming the glorious ones" is then likened to those humans of Sodom and Gomorrah who sexually "pursued strange flesh" by trying to copulate with angels (v.7). Divine beings are often described as shining with brilliance and glory in both the Old Testament (Ezekiel 1:4–7, 27–28; Daniel 10:6) as well as the New Testament (Matthew 28:3; Luke 24:4).

Lastly, Michael is referenced again as the archangel who fights with his angels against the satanic dragon and his angels in Revelation 12.

> Revelation 12:7–8:
> Now war arose in heaven, Michael and his angels fighting against the dragon. And the dragon and his angels fought back, but he was defeated, and there was no longer any place for them in heaven.

I write about this momentous spiritual event in my series Chronicles of the Apocalypse (paid link).

Though both Old and New Testament only names Michael as the Watcher, or guardian angel, of God's people and Gabriel as his "wingman," Second Temple Jewish apocalypticism maintained a strong tradition that there are seven named archangels, four of whom stand in God's presence: Michael, Gabriel, Raphael, and Uriel (sometimes called Phanuel). The other three are named Raguel, Saraqael, and Remiel (1 Enoch 20:1-7; Tobit 12:15).

Though not as explicit, Revelation 8:2 mentions "seven angels who stand before God," and Gabriel describes himself also as "standing before God" (Luke 1:19), the same phrase used of the archangels in the Second Temple tradition (1 Enoch 40:3; Tobit 12:15).

Thus, I followed this archangelic tradition throughout all my Chronicles series, including Chronicles of the Watchers.

Chapter 4: Cosmic Geography

Underworld Valleys

In the novel *Jezebel: Harlot Queen of Israel*, there is a sequence where Baal travels to Jerusalem but is trapped by the archangels in the Valley of Hinnom just outside the city walls. It is here at the infamous location of the tophet of Molech where Baal is swallowed up in a sinkhole as the jaws of Mot takes him down into the underworld of Sheol. While we have already discussed Mot above and will further discuss Sheol below, let's take a look at the notion of valleys as connections to the underworld in the Bible and in the ancient Near East.[1]

Critical Bible scholar Francesca Stavrakopoulou explains that, as the holy city, Jerusalem's sacred topography is mapped onto the biblical cosmos of a three-tiered universe: the heavens above where divinity resides, the earth below for humankind, and the underworld of the dead beneath it all. The mountain is the transition between heaven and earth. It's where temples of the gods reside like the temple of Yahweh on Mount Zion. The valleys, therefore, operate in a similar manner as the transition or points of entry from the earth into the underworld—like the Valley of Hinnom on the southwest side of Jerusalem.

> As sites of transition, the valleys surrounding Jerusalem are thus imbued with a potent mytho-symbolic character; they are liminal locations marking at once three interrelated places: the transitional place between the ordered city and the uncultivated wilderness, the roots of the holy hill upon

---

[1] Special thanks to Robert Cruickshank for finding some of the scholarship presented here on Underworld valleys.

which the heavenly and earthly realms meet, and the intersection of the earthly realm and the underworld.[2]

The Second-Temple Jewish text of 1 Enoch uses this image of the valley as a place of judgment that ends in the underworld.

> 1 Enoch 53:1-3:
> My eyes saw there a valley with a wide and deep mouth. And all those who dwell upon the earth, the sea, and the islands shall bring to it gifts, presents, and tributes; yet this deep valley shall not become full… Sinners shall be destroyed from before the face of the Lord of the Spirits—they shall perish eternally, standing before the face of his earth.[3]

The first sentence about the valley of judgment uses the language of Mot (Death) as the wide and deep mouth that is never satisfied ("shall not become full"). The idea here is that the valley is a place of judgment where sinners meet their destruction ("perish"). In 1 Enoch, valleys are places of judgment that lead to Sheol, like the mouth of Mot.

Then Enoch sees another valley of judgment where kings are judged in connection with the angelic Watchers who rule over them.

> 1 Enoch 54:1-2:
>
> Then I looked and turned to another face of the earth and saw there a valley, deep and burning with fire. And they were bringing kings and potentates and were throwing them into this deep valley. And my eyes saw there their chains while they were making them into iron fetters of immense weight. And I asked the angel of peace, who was going with me, saying, "For whom are these imprisonment chains being prepared?" And he said unto me, "These are being prepared for the armies of Azaz'el [the Watchers], in order that they

---

[2] Francesca Stavrakopoulou, "The Jerusalem Tophet: Ideological Dispute and Religious Transformation," *Studi Epigrafici e Linguistici* 29-30, 2012-2013: 141.

[3] James H. Charlesworth, *The Old Testament Pseudepigrapha, vol. 1* (New York; London: Yale University Press, 1983), 37. Thanks to Robert Cruickshank for finding this passage.

may take them and cast them into the abyss of complete condemnation.[45]

So the valley of judgment leads to the Abyss of Sheol where earthly and heavenly rulers and powers are cast down for judgment to be imprisoned and punished later. Another linking of valleys with the underworld.

In the Old Testament, several texts point to this same idea of valleys as portals to the underworld. The first one is a prophecy by Isaiah that reflects the same concept as the 1 Enoch passages above.

> Isaiah 24:21–22:
> On that day the LORD will punish the host of heaven, in
> heaven, and the kings of the earth, on the earth. They will be
> gathered together as prisoners in a pit; they will be shut up
> in a prison, and after many days they will be punished.

Though the word "valley" is not used here, the prophetic picture is almost a mirror description of Enoch's prophecy of earthly and heavenly rulers and powers being cast down into a pit to be imprisoned and punished later.

Secondly, there is a valley just outside of Jerusalem called Valley of the Rephaim (2 Samuel 5:22).[6] In Canaanite mythology, the Rephaim were divinized dead warrior kings, heroes of the past, who were called up from the underworld to legitimize current rulers.[7] Another valley linked with the underworld. We'll explore the Rephaim in more detail under Chapter 5, the "marzeah feast."

The third example of underworld valleys is the Valley of Hinnom at the southwest walls of Jerusalem. As shown in the novel, this valley was the location of a Tophet altar of Molech where children were sacrificed by being "burned with fire" (Jeremiah 7:31). Because this idolatrous practice was so

---

[4] James H. Charlesworth, *The Old Testament Pseudepigrapha*, vol. 1 (New York; London: Yale University Press, 1983), 38.

[5] Charlesworth, *Old Testament Pseudepigrapha*, vol. 1, 38.

[6] See also Josh 15:8; 2 Sam 23:13; 1 Chron 11:15; 14:9; Isaiah17:5.

[7] Nick Wyatt, "À la recherche des Rephaïm perdus", *The Archaeology of Myth*, ed. Nick Wyatt, (London: Equinox, 2010) , 587-588.

abominable to Yahweh, Jeremiah prophesied destruction upon Jerusalem so devastating it would fill the valley with dead corpses and lead to the Babylonian exile of death (7:33). The name of the Valley of Hinnom would be changed to the Valley of Slaughter (7:32).

> Jeremiah 7:32–33:
> Behold, the days are coming, declares the LORD, when it will no more be called Topheth, or the Valley of the Son of Hinnom, but the Valley of Slaughter; for they will bury in Topheth, because there is no room elsewhere. And the dead bodies of this people will be food for the birds of the air, and for the beasts of the earth.

During the Hellenistic development of the Second Temple period, "the Valley of Hinnom, often referred to simply as 'the accursed valley' or 'abyss,' then came to represent the place of eschatological judgment of wicked Jews by fire (1 Enoch. 26–27; 54:1–6; 56:1–4; 90:24–27)… Gehenna had become hell itself."[8]

When Ezekiel predicted the destruction of Gog in his major eschatological prophecy, he declared that it would occur in a valley that is tied to the underworld:

> Ezekiel 39:11:
> "On that day I will give to Gog a place for burial in Israel, the Valley of the Travelers, east of the sea. It will block the travelers, for there Gog and all his multitude will be buried. It will be called the Valley of Hamon-gog.

"Valley of the Travelers" in Hebrew is *Valley of the Oberim*. That name is not about mere travelers on the roads and valleys. Bible commentator Daniel Block explains the underworld valley connection best as a designation for "those who have passed on," in other words, deceased heroes that are referred to elsewhere as Rephaim.

---

[8] Duane F. Watson, "Gehenna (Place)," ed. David Noel Freedman, *The Anchor Yale Bible Dictionary* (New York: Doubleday, 1992), 927.

This netherworldly connection may hold the key to this frame as a whole. Gog and his warriors have imagined themselves to be like the nobles of old, but Yahweh hereby declares their doom. They are sentenced to death just as Egypt and all his companions in ch. 32…When the corpses of Gog and his horde are gathered, the pile in the "valley of those who have passed on" will be completely blocked off, that is, filled, so it will hold no more bodies. Sixth, because of its new usage, the site will receive a new name, *gê' hămôn gôg*, "the Valley of Hamon-Gog," which appears to play on *gê' hinnōm*, "the valley of Hinnom." Earlier this was the site of Molech worship and child sacrifice (e.g., Jeremiah 2:23), and the place where the bodies of animals and criminals were burned.[9]

Block also points out that "east of the sea" presumably meant the Mediterranean Sea and that the mass burial was suggestive of this important locale being reduced to a common cemetery. Notice also the linguistic connection to that other underworld Valley of Hinnom, which would become the ultimate symbol of judgment.

You might remember those victory feasts we mentioned earlier of eating Leviathan in the desert of Sinai (Psalm 74:14), birds consuming the enemies of Jesus in the marriage supper of the Lamb (Revelations 19:17-18), and Jeremiah's slaughter (Jeremiah 7:33). Ezekiel's prophecy has such a feast as well.

> Ezekiel 39:17–18:
> Thus says the Lord GOD: "Speak to the birds of every sort and to all beasts of the field: 'Assemble and come, gather from all around to the sacrificial feast that I am preparing for you, a great sacrificial feast on the mountains of Israel, and you shall eat flesh and drink blood. You shall eat the flesh of the mighty, and drink the blood of the princes of the earth— of rams, of lambs, and of he-goats, of bulls, all of them fat beasts of Bashan.'"

---

[9] Daniel Isaac Block, *The Book of Ezekiel, Chapters 25–48*, The New International Commentary on the Old Testament (Grand Rapids, MI: Wm. B. Eerdmans Publishing Co., 1997–), 468–470.

The birds would feast on Gog as a memorial of God's destruction of his enemies. The valley would be a valley of death—in Israel. But notice that last word. The beasts being eaten would be "fat beasts of Bashan." Bashan was a deeply significant spiritual location to the Canaanites and the Hebrews. As the *DDD* puts it, biblical geographical tradition agrees with the mythological and cultic data of the Canaanites of Ugarit that "the Bashan region, or a part of it, clearly represented 'Hell', the celestial and infernal abode of their deified dead kings," i.e., the Rephaim.[10]

Mount Hermon was in Bashan, and Mount Hermon was a location in the Bible linked to the Rephaim and ruled over by Og (Joshua 12:1–5). But it was also the legendary location where the heavenly Sons of God were considered to have come to earth in rebellion before the Flood.[11]

The underworld connections just keep growing. But we'll stop there and jump into the abyss of that underworld, which is the next cosmic geographical location: Sheol.

Sheol

Sheol was the Hebrew word for the underworld.[12] Though the Bible doesn't contain any narratives of experiences in Sheol, it was nevertheless described as the abode of the dead that was below the earth. Sheol was sometimes used interchangeably with Abaddon as the place of destruction of the body (Proverbs 15:11; 27:20),[13] and the grave as a reference to the state of being dead and buried in the earth (Psalm 88:11; Isaiah 14:9-11). But it was also considered to be *physically* located beneath the earth.

---

[10] "Bashan," *DDD*, p 161-162. "According to *KTU* 1.108:1–3, the abode of the dead and deified king, and his place of enthronement as *[Rephaim]* was in *[Ashtarot and Edrei]*, in amazing correspondence with the Biblical tradition about the seat of king Og of Bashan, "one of the survivors of the Rephaim, who lived in Ashtarot and Edrei" (Josh 12:4)."

[11] The non-canonical book of Enoch supports this same interpretation: "Enoch 6:6 And they were in all two hundred [sons of God]; who descended in the days of Jared on the summit of Mount Hermon, and they called it Mount Hermon, because they had sworn and bound themselves by mutual imprecations upon it."

[12] "Sheol," *DDD*, p 768.

[13] "Abaddon," *DDD*, p 1.

When the sons of Korah were swallowed up by the earth for their rebellion against God, Numbers chapter 16 says that "they <u>went down alive into Sheol</u>, and the earth closed over them, and they perished from the midst of the assembly" (v. 33). People would not "fall alive" into death or the grave and then perish if Sheol wasn't a location. But they would die after they fell down into a location (Sheol) and the earth closed over them in that order.

The divine being (*elohim*), known as the departed spirit of Samuel, "came up out of the earth" for the witch of Endor's necromancy with Saul (1 Samuel 28:13). This wasn't a reference to a body coming out of a grave, but a spirit of the dead coming from the underworld beneath the earth.

When Isaiah writes about Sheol in Isaiah 14, he combines the notion of the physical location of the dead body in the earth (v. 11) with the location beneath the earth of the spirits of the dead (v. 9). It's really a both/and proposition.

> Isaiah 14:9, 11:
> <u>Sheol beneath</u> is stirred up to meet you when you come; it <u>rouses the shades</u> to greet you…Your pomp is <u>brought down to Sheol</u>.

Here is a list of some verses that speak of Sheol geographically as an underworld habitation for spirits in contrast with heaven as an overworld habitation for spirits.

> Amos 9:2:
> "If they <u>dig into Sheol</u>, from there shall my hand take them; if they climb <u>up to heaven</u>, from there I will bring them down.

> Job 11:8 :
> It is <u>higher than heaven</u>—what can you do? <u>Deeper than Sheol</u>—what can you know?

> Psalm 139:8:
> If I <u>ascend to heaven</u>, you are there! If I make my <u>bed in Sheol</u>, you are there!

Isaiah 7:11:
Ask a sign of the LORD your God; let it be <u>deep as Sheol</u> or <u>high as heaven</u>."

These are not mere references to the body in the grave but to locations of the spiritual soul as well. Sheol and heaven are a dichotomous totality of geographical opposites. As the above verses attest, they are shown in the Bible to be opposing locations. Sheol is a combined term that describes both the grave for the body and the underworld location of the departed souls of the dead.

In the New Testament, the word Hades is used for the underworld, which was the Greek equivalent of Sheol.[14] Jesus himself used the term Hades as the location of damned spirits in contrast with heaven as the location of redeemed spirits when he talked of Capernaum at the judgment, "And you, Capernaum, will you be <u>exalted to heaven</u>? You will be <u>brought down to Hades</u>" (Matthew 11:23).

Hades/Sheol was also the location of *all* departed spirits in his parable of Lazarus and the rich man in Hades (Luke 16:19-31).

In the novel *Jezebel: Harlot Queen of Israel*, I tell the story of Anat going into Sheol to find her brother Baal, held hostage by Mot in his city of Death. There is no detailed depiction of Sheol in the Old Testament, and while the picture of the Greek Hades is commonly used in fiction, I chose instead to use the only Jewish picture of the underworld that I could find because it would be the closest Hebrew understanding to the Bible. Granted, it isn't canonical but only an imaginative construction of a spiritual reality.

Though 1 Enoch is not Scripture, I have argued elsewhere for the high regard that the New Testament gives the ancient text as a source for some of its own theological concepts and language.[15] The revered ancient Jewish book consists of several "books" that recount an expanded version of the Genesis 6 story of the Watchers and Nephilim giants as well as visions the prophet Enoch allegedly experienced. In these visions, angels take Enoch around the earth, up into the heights of heaven, and down into the depths of Hades (which are

---

[14] "Hades," *DDD*, p 382.

[15] See the chapter "The Book of Enoch: Scripture, Heresy, or What?" in *When Giants Were Upon the Earth: The Watchers, Nephilim and the Cosmic War of the Seed* (Los Angeles: Embedded Pictures, 2014).

actually arrived at by going to the "ends of the earth" rather than descending down into the earth). Unfortunately, these visions are obscure, overlapping, and at times contradictory, so scholars have disagreed over their interpretation as well as their actual cosmic geography. I have attempted to use my own reading of the text and to integrate it with several of these scholarly viewpoints that can be found analyzed in the book *A Study of the Geography of 1 Enoch 17-19* by Kelley Coblentz Bautch.[16] Imagination is required!

Since Enoch's "map" is cosmic, it includes Sheol/Hades as well as the heavens and the earth. But some scholars have argued that Enoch's entire journey is to the realm of the dead.[17] So I decided to use the ancient Near Eastern (and Jewish) notion of "on earth as it is in heaven" (Matthew 6:10) or "as above, so below," to apply to the underworld as well. In this way, the geography of Hades is a reflection of the sacred geography of the earth above ("sacred geography" means that it doesn't so much follow physical geography as it does theological meaning).

Since the underworld was believed by the Jews to be under the earth[18] and accessed by the waters of the Abyss,[19] which was the source of the waters above,[20] I have those waters work as a kind of sky in the dome of the underworld (though not in all places). The mountains below rise up from Hades to the earth above. So Mount Zion in Hades rises up and penetrates the ceiling of Hades and becomes Mount Zion on earth above them. This fulfills the ancient Near Eastern notion of the cosmic mountains being an *axis mundi*, a connection between the heavens, the earth and the underworld.[21]

The circle of Hades matches the circle of the earth above it and likewise has an ocean/river (the Great Sea or Abyss) at its outer reaches that extends

---

[16] Kelley Coblentz Bautch, *A Study of the Geography of 1 Enoch 17-19: No One Has Seen What I Have Seen*, (Leiden, Netherlands: Brill, 2003).

[17] Glasson, T. Francis. Greek Influence in Jewish Eschatology. London: S.P.C.K., 1961, 8-11; Nickelsburg, *Jewish Literature between the Bible and the Mishnah*, (Philadelphia: Fortress Press, 1981) 54–55; 66, n. 26; also *1 Enoch*, 280; James C. VanderKam, *Enoch and the Growth of an Apocalyptic Tradition*. CBQMS 16. Washington, D.C.: Catholic Biblical Association of America, 1984.

[18] Amos 9:2.

[19] Ps. 136:6; Job 41:34 LXX.

[20] Wayne Horowitz, *Mesopotamian Cosmic Geography*, (Winona Lake; IN: Eisenbrauns, 1998), 334-348.

[21] Richard J. Clifford, *The Cosmic Mountain in Canaan and the Old Testament* (Wipf & Stock Pub, 2010). Also, Isa. 14:13-15.

beyond the "Four Winds" or "Four Corners" of the earth where the pillars of the earth support the heavens and the earth (1 Enoch 17:5; Proverbs 8:27, 29; 1 Samuel 2:8; Mark 13:27).[22]

In this conceptual map, Jerusalem, or Mount Zion, is at the center of the earth, and has "the accursed valley" (Gehenna) right next to it (Ezekiel 5:5, 38:12; 1 Enoch 26:1-2; 27:2).

North from that center resides Mount Hermon, the "rock" (mountain) upon which Jesus said God would build his new kingdom church.[23] This mountain is described as "reaching to the heavens" and as being the celestial storehouse of the luminaries and storms (1 Enoch 17:3). Many rivers flow from it, including a river of fire and a river of "living waters" (17:4-8), and it is guarded by fiery beings who take human shape (17:1). This "source of the waters" is a reflection of the cosmic Mountain of Eden and its source of living waters (Ezekiel 28:13-14).[24]

In the south are seven mountains of precious stones arranged in a perpendicular layout. The central mountain burns with fire day and night and is called the "throne of God," where God will come down at the final judgment. These elements suggest it is Mount Sinai (1 Enoch 24-25).

In the west are "wintery winds" and the "great darkness," where another mountain hosts "hollow places" for the souls of all the dead. The righteous are separated from the sinners, much like the chasm separates the righteous in Abraham's Bosom from the sinners in the parable of Lazarus. (Luke 16:19-26; 1 Enoch 17:6; 22:1-14).

In the east are "great beasts and birds" at the ends of the earth (1 Enoch 33:1). Tartarus is further "beyond the edge of the earth," where the earth meets to uphold the vault of heaven (1 Enoch 18:10).[25] This is where the angels who sinned in Genesis 6 were kept imprisoned in gloomy darkness (2 Peter 2:4; 1 Peter 3:18-20). They were in deep pits or chasms that are like fiery pillars. (1 Enoch 18:10-16).

---

[22] See also Isa. 40:22; Zech. 9:10; Job 38:4.

[23] Matt. 16:18.

[24] Bautch, *A Study of the Geography of 1 Enoch*, 64-69.

[25] George W. E. Nickelsburg, *1 Enoch: A Commentary on the Book of 1 Enoch*, ed. Klaus Baltzer, *Hermeneia—a Critical and Historical Commentary on the Bible* (Minneapolis, MN: Fortress, 2001), 286.

There is much more detail that can be quite confusing to follow, so I have included an illustrated map with some of the major elements adapted from Bautch and my own reading of 1Enoch.

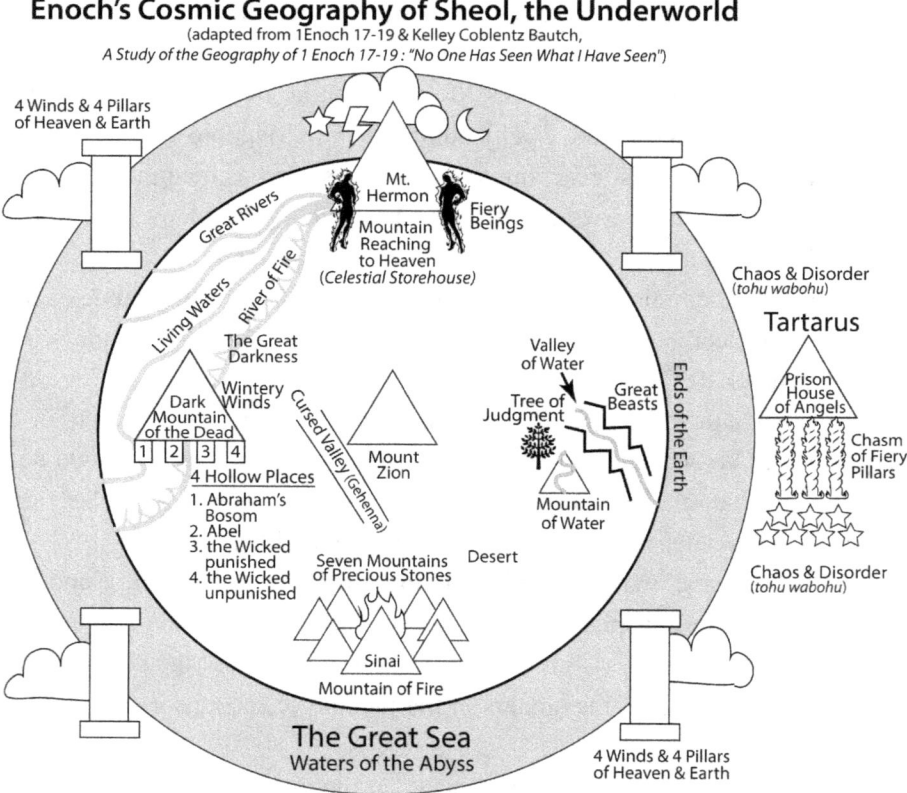

Cosmic Mountains

In the novel *Jezebel: Harlot Queen of Israel*, several mountains become significant locations of divinity and play heavily into the spiritual storyline. They incarnate the notion of a cosmic mountain, or holy mountain, a location where heaven and earth are connected, where deities reside in temples or tents, and where the source waters of life often pour forth. This symbolic imagery has been carried through from the two series *Chronicles of the Nephilim* and

Chronicles of the Apocalypse (paid links) because it is a key feature of the ancient worldview of cosmic geography.

The confrontation between Elijah and Jezebel's prophets of Baal takes place on Mount Carmel, a holy mountain that Baalists had taken as booty from Israel earlier in history. They had torn down an altar of Yahweh that was originally there and replaced it with an altar to Baal. Yahweh took it back with fire from heaven.

Baal has his own cosmic Mount Saphon in the north where, according to the Baal epic, he built his palace after achieving priority among the gods. This actual mountain is in Syria, 180 miles north of Tyre.

Mount Hermon is known as the location where the Watchers fell to earth before the Flood, and it remained the location of their divine council or assembly of rebels to that day. In its foothills was the infamous "Gates of Hades" in the cave of Panias that led into the Abyss. Yes, those "Gates of Hades" that Jesus referred to.

When Elijah became bereft and lost his way spiritually, he journeyed to Mount Sinai, the holy mountain of Yahweh, where the Torah was delivered amidst the divine council of heavenly host. Jerusalem, the location of Yahweh's temple, is referred to as Mount Zion, the new holy mountain that ultimately replaced Sinai as Yahweh's abode.

Biblical scholar Richard Clifford explains the concept of holy mountains or cosmic mountains playing an important role in the religious thought of the ancient Near East, including Israel: "In this view, heaven and earth united were seen as a mountain. The base of the mountain was the earth and the peak was the top of the heavens. Thus the mountain was the central axis of the universe and was the connecting point between the different spheres."[26]

The connections run deep between Canaanite and Israelite cosmic mountains. In Ugaritic mythology, the high god El lived in a tent on his holy mountain and counseled with his heavenly host, the seventy Sons of God.[27] At Sinai, Yahweh dwelt in a tent (tabernacle) at the foot of his holy mountain, where he counseled with his heavenly host and gave his decrees to the people

---

[26] Richard J. Clifford, *The Cosmic Mountain in Canaan and the Old Testament* (Wipf & Stock Pub, 2010),190.

[27] Clifford, *The Cosmic Mountain*, 124-125. Seventy Sons of Asherah: page 61.

(Deuteronomy 33:1-2; Psalm 68:15-17). In Hebrew, one of God's names is El Shaddai, whose translation most likely means "God of the mountain."[28] By the time of Solomon's temple, the new location for Yahweh's dwelling, Jerusalem, had become designated Mount Zion, the holy mountain "in the heights of the north" (Psalm 48:1-2). I'll explain what "heights of the north" (*sapon*) means below. But for now, notice that this new holy mountain of Zion is poetically linked to Eden, described as "the holy mountain" in Ezekiel 28:13-16. God's presence is linked to mountains from Eden to Sinai to Zion, just as pagan deities claimed mountains as their own.

In fact, one could say that the Bible records a battle of cosmic mountains between Yahweh and others like Baal. Certain scriptures point toward God taking over the enemy's mountain as his own and building his city of victory upon it.

One element of Baal's reign was his mountain abode of Mount Saphon (various spellings include Zaphon, Sapan, Sapon). A plethora of Ugaritic texts link Baal with his "divine mountain, Saphon/Sapan."[29] He is said to be buried there[30] in his sanctuary[31] on the mountain of victory.[32]

In Isaiah 14:13, Isaiah mocks the arrogance of the king of Babylon by likening him to another mythological figure, Athtar, who sought to take Baal's throne and failed "on the mountain of assembly on the summit of Zaphon [Sapan]."[33]

In the Bible, this Mount Zaphon of Baal is subverted by Israel's holy Mount Zion.

> Psalm 48:1–2:
> Great is the LORD and greatly to be praised in the city of our God! His holy mountain, beautiful in elevation, is the joy of

---

[28] Gordon J. Wenham, "The Religion of the Patriarchs," A.R. Millard & D.J. Wiseman, eds., *Essays on the Patriarchal Narratives*. Leicester: IVP, 1980, pp.157-188.

[29] KTU 1.101:1-9; 1.100:9; 1.3:3:29.

[30] KTU 1.6:1:15-18.

[31] KTU 1.3:3:30.

[32] KTU 1.101:1-4.

[33] Michael Heiser, "The Mythological Provenance of Isaiah 14:12-15: A Reconsideration of the Ugaritic Material" Liberty University http://digitalcommons.liberty.edu/lts_fac_pubs/280

all the earth, Mount Zion, in the far north [*zaphon*], the city
of the great King.

In this scripture the holy Mount Zion is described as being in "the far north," the very location of Baal's Mount Saphon (Zaphon), but not in fact the actual location of Israel's Mount Zion. So "the far north" is a theological, not a geographical designation of Zion replacing Saphon as the divine mountain par excellence.[34]

But God's battle over mountains is far from complete. He also speaks about Mount Hermon, known as "mountain of Bashan," as being a target for conquering. The region of Bashan was translated as "place of the serpent," the area where Og of Bashan ruled, the last of the Rephaim, those warriors connected to the underworld.[35] Mount Hermon of Bashan was the location where the Watchers came to earth and made their evil covenant in their diabolical divine assembly.

The origin story of the Watchers is partially revealed in Genesis 6:1-4, where the angelic Sons of God came to earth before the Flood. They mated with humans in violation of God's heavenly and earthly divide. This is one of the reasons why God sent the Flood and imprisoned those beings in Tartarus (2 Peter 2:4-5; Jude 6).

> Genesis 6:1–3
> When man began to multiply on the face of the land and
> daughters were born to them, the sons of God saw that the
> daughters of man were attractive. And they took as their
> wives any they chose.

I've given extensive biblical and historical evidence for this supernatural angelic incursion and its evil results in my book *When Giants Were Upon the Earth (paid link)*, so I will save room here. What I want to point out is that

---

[34] H. Niehr, "Zaphon", in *Dictionary of Deities and Demons in the Bible*, ed. Karel van der Toorn, Bob Becking and Pieter W. van der Horst, 2nd extensively rev. ed., 929 (Leiden; Boston; Köln; Grand Rapids, MI; Cambridge: Brill; Eerdmans, 1999). Also see Job 26:7; 37:22; Ezek. 1:4 where the word "north" is used as a spiritual reference, more allusion to the divine mountain Saphon of Canaanite belief.

[35] Michael S. Heiser, *The Unseen Realm: Recovering the Supernatural Worldview of the Bible*, First Edition (Bellingham, WA: Lexham Press, 2015), 200.

Genesis doesn't tell us *where* these Sons of God (aka Watchers) came down to earth. But there is an ancient book that does. This is the writings of 1 Enoch, a non-canonical Jewish text that expands on Genesis 6.

I also argued in my *Giants* book that 1 Enoch is not Scripture, but it was quoted and paraphrased in the New Testament books of 1 John, Jude, 2 Peter, and others,[36] so it certainly deserves the respect that the historic Christian church had given it until the modern era.

In it, we read of the Genesis 6 "sons of God," called "sons of heaven" in 1 Enoch, making a covenant with one another to come to earth and "choose wives for themselves from among the daughters of men" to beget children, just like Genesis 6 says. Here's how it happens.

> 1 Enoch 6:3-6:
> And Semyaz, being their leader, said unto them, "I fear that perhaps you will not consent that this deed should be done, and I alone will become (responsible) for this great sin." But they all responded to him, "Let us all swear an oath and bind everyone among us by a curse not to abandon this suggestion but to do the deed." Then they all swore together and bound one another by (the curse). And they were altogether two hundred; and they descended into 'Ardos, which is the summit of Hermon. And they called the mount Armon, for they swore and bound one another by a curse.[37]

1 Enoch is called the Book of the Watchers, and these "angels" in this passage are elsewhere called "Watchers of heaven who have abandoned the high heaven, the holy eternal place, and have defiled themselves with women" (1 Enoch 12:4).[38] Of course there are many aspects to discuss about this story. But for our purposes here, notice that these fallen Watchers swear an oath of covenant in their assembly on the mountain, like a diabolical inversion of

---

[36] See the chapter "The Book of Enoch: Scripture, Heresy, or What?" in Brian Godawa, *When Giants Were Upon the Earth: The Watchers, Nephilim and the Cosmic War of the Seed* (Los Angeles: Embedded Pictures, 2014), 24-37.

[37] James H. Charlesworth, *The Old Testament Pseudepigrapha*, vol. 1 (New York; London: Yale University Press, 1983), 15.

[38] See also 1 Enoch 10:9, 15; 13:10; 14:1-3; chapters 15 and 16.

Yahweh's sworn covenant with Israel on Mount Sinai. Hermon became their "mount of assembly," from which they invaded the earth (1 Enoch 13:7).

An enigmatic Greek inscription from the third century A.D. found at the peak of Mount Hermon coincides quite eerily with this Watcher oath. It reads, "According to the command of the greatest and holy God, those who take an oath proceed from here."[39]

From primeval days, Mount Hermon was Ground Zero, the headquarters of rebellion against Yahweh, the original evil cosmic mountain. And that mountain was located in Bashan, "land of the serpent," residence of the last of the Rephaim monsters who defied Yahweh as well. That cosmic mountain of Bashan, known as Mount Hermon, would become the symbolic mountain of power that Yahweh would ultimately defeat and own. He said so in Psalm 68.

> Psalm 68:15–22:
> O mountain of God, mountain of Bashan;
> > O many-peaked mountain, mountain of Bashan!
> Why do you look with hatred, O many-peaked mountain,
> > at the mount that God desired for his abode,
> > yes, where the LORD will dwell forever?
> The chariots of God are twice ten thousand,
> > thousands upon thousands;
> > the Lord is among them; Sinai is now in the sanctuary.
> You ascended on high,
> > leading a host of captives in your train
> > and receiving gifts among men,
> even among the rebellious, that the LORD God may dwell there…
> But God will strike the heads of his enemies...

---

[39] George W. E. Nickelsburg, *1 Enoch: A Commentary on the Book of 1 Enoch*, ed. Klaus Baltzer, *Hermeneia—a Critical and Historical Commentary on the Bible* (Minneapolis, MN: Fortress, 2001), 247.

"In addition to the oath, which is reminiscent of the oath of the watchers in 1 Enoch 6:6, the title "the greatest and holy God" closely parallels one of 1 Enoch's favorite divine titles, "the Great Holy One," often rendered into Greek as "the Great and Holy One" (see comm. on 1:3c–4). The similarities might reflect cultic activity that was somehow informed by traditions from 1 Enoch…

"Two final attestations concerning the sacred character of Hermon occur in the church fathers. In the Onomasticon, Eusebius says of the mountain that "it is honored as sacred by the gentiles." Interpreting this, Jerome states, "At its peak is a noted temple that is reverenced by the Gentiles from the region of Paneas and Lebanon."

Nickelsburg, *1 Enoch*, 247.

> The Lord said, "I will bring them back from Bashan,
> I will bring them back from the depths of the sea."

In this psalm, God takes ownership of Bashan with his heavenly host of warriors, but then replaces it and refers to Mount Sinai (soon to be Zion). It isn't that God is making Bashan his mountain literally, but conquering its divinities and theologically replacing it with his new cosmic mountain elsewhere.

In verse 18, Yahweh leads captives in triumphal procession and receives tribute from them as spoils of war (v. 18). Paul quoted this very verse to be a reference to Christ's ascension and his victory over the spiritual powers.

> Ephesians 4:8–10:
> Therefore it says, "When he ascended on high he led a host
> of captives, and he gave gifts to men."
> (In saying "he ascended," what does it mean but that he had
> also descended into the lower regions, the earth? He who
> descended is the one who also ascended far above all the
> heavens, that he might fill all things.)

Yahweh will own and live where once the rebellious ruled (v. 18). He will strike his enemies' heads and bring them all out from the sea of chaos, that wilderness where Leviathan symbolically reigns.

This battle of cosmic mountains is the foundation that finally gives meaning to the famous passage about Jesus building his Church upon a "rock" in Matthew 16.

> Matthew 16:18:
> And I tell you, you are Peter, and on this rock I will build my
> church, and the gates of Hades shall not prevail against it.

Ironically, both Roman Catholics and Protestants are wrong when they interpret this passage. Roman Catholics think that Jesus is referring to Peter as the first pope, as though he was making a word play with Peter meaning "stone" like a "rock." But of course it would be complete and utter nonsense, not to mention blasphemy, for Jesus, the Son of God, sinless God in the flesh, to build his glorious kingdom Church upon a sinful human being rather than upon himself as sinless high priest and savior of that Church.

But Protestants are equally wrong to argue that the "rock" is Peter's confession of Christ's Sonship, for the location where they were standing when Jesus uttered those words was at a sacred place literally called "The Gates of Hades" believed to lead down to the Abyss.[40]

The rock Jesus was referring to was Mount Hermon, in whose foothills they were standing. Jesus was fulfilling the promise of Psalm 68 noted above that Yahweh would conquer the cosmic mountain of Bashan, Mount Hermon, the mountain that was God's rival, the cosmic mountain that represented spiritual rebellion. By creating his Church, the spiritual Mount Zion and its heavenly Jerusalem (Hebrews 12:22), Jesus was then building his victorious kingdom upon the spiritual ruins of that wretched, rebellious "rock" before which they were standing.

With his resurrection and ascension, Jesus as Messiah took back Mount Hermon and was installed as "king upon Zion, God's holy mountain" (Psalm 2:6). Read more detailed exposition of that theological victory of Christ at the Gates of Hades in my book *When Giants Were Upon the Earth (paid link)*.

---

[40] *Wars of the Jews* 1:405, Flavius Josephus and William Whiston, The Works of Josephus: Complete and Unabridged (Peabody: Hendrickson, 1987).

Chapter 5:
Cultic Practice

High Places

When the Israelites first entered the Promised Land to dispossess the Canaanites, Yahweh told them to destroy the altars where the pagans worshipped their gods "on the high mountains and on the hills and under every green tree" (Deuteronomy 12:2-6). This phrase would become a meme for what was called "high places" (Hebrew: *bamah*; plural: *bamot*).[1] The Israelites were told to tear down the altars and chop down and dash into pieces the images of the gods that Canaanites worshipped.

Archaeological digs have uncovered some of these high places throughout the land. They were usually locations of cultic sacrifice that were elevated, either naturally on a hill or artificially on large open-air stone platforms with stairs. Some had large sacred pillars called *massebot* in Hebrew (to be discussed below), asherim poles, and other images of gods. Some were simple sanctuaries. Others were entire complexes of worship that included a courtyard and a dining hall for sacred meals (1 Samuel 9:25) as well as various side rooms, not unlike the temple complex in Jerusalem.[2]

Upon first entering the Land of Canaan, the Israelites were told to create their own high places to worship Yahweh with simple earth or unhewn stone rather than the large platforms that typified Canaanite worship (Exodus 20:24-26). Israel was to be different. Before the temple was built, Yahweh approved of the high places created exclusively for him. David worshipped Yahweh

---

[1] 1 Kings. 14:23; 2 Kings. 16:4; 17:10; Jer. 3:6.

[2] Philip J. King, Lawrence E. Stager, *Life in Biblical Israel* (Louisville, KY: Westminster John Knox Press, 2001), 320.

with a priesthood at the high place in Gibeon according to God's own commands.

> 1 Chronicles 16:39–40:
> And [David] left Zadok the priest and his brothers the priests before the tabernacle of the LORD in the high place that was at Gibeon to offer burnt offerings to the LORD on the altar of burnt offering regularly morning and evening, to do all that is written in the Law of the LORD that he commanded Israel.

Solomon too served Yahweh at the main high place (out of many) in Gibeon. But once the king built the temple of Yahweh in Jerusalem, the high places were no longer legitimate locations to worship Yahweh (1 Kings 3:2-4). All worship was to be centralized in the single house of God in Jerusalem.

But the king and his people both failed to obey this command of God. Solomon himself built high places to the gods Molech and Chemosh just outside the walls of Jerusalem (1 Kings 11:7). When the kingdom split after Solomon, Jeroboam placed two golden calves in both Dan and Bethel in high place complexes (1 Kings 12:31).

The high places in both Israel and Judah were never destroyed until the time of King Hezekiah in the eighth century (2 Kings 18:4), *over two hundred years after Solomon's temple was built.* Two hundred years of widespread usage of forbidden high places. And even then, many high places were left in Judah until King Josiah's more thorough reforms seventy five years later. Josiah was the one credited with the most significant elimination of idolatry in Judah and Israel. He destroyed the high places outside Jerusalem along with all their constituent elements of altars, asherim, and sacred pillars, as well as the abominable Tophet of Molech in the Valley of Hinnom and the unholy vessels of idol worship in Yahweh's temple (2 Kings 23).

The Scripture sings praise of Josiah.

> 2 Kings 23:25:
> Before [Josiah] there was no king like him, who turned to the LORD with all his heart and with all his soul and with all his might, according to all the Law of Moses, nor did any like him arise after him.

Yet in spite of this momentary righteousness of Josiah, *all the next four kings of Judah* "did evil in the sight of the Lord," bringing a return to the abominable worship of Canaanite gods and polluting Yahweh's house in Jerusalem that had previously been cleansed (2 Chronicles 36:14).

The ancient Jews simply wouldn't give up their high places and addiction to the spiritual infidelity of worshipping other gods.

Standing Stones

We've already discussed the wooden poles called asherim above. These were ubiquitous images related to the goddess Asherah that were closely linked with altars of both Baal and Yahweh at high places throughout Israel and Judah.

Another common element of the high place were sacred pillars, or *massebot* (singular: *massebah*). These were standing stone slabs from a few feet to ten feet tall that stood upright. Though pillars like this, also called *stela*, were used for various purposes such as boundary markers and victory memorials, Canaanites also erected such stela as markers for the presence of deified ancestors.[3] In the Old Testament, the term *massebah*, when used for cultic purposes, was nearly always a reference to standing stones "erected to commemorate the appearance or presence of a deity."[4]

Archaeologist Ziony Zevit describes the language related to these standing stones or pillars. They were "made from stone" (Genesis 22:18; 31:13; Exodus 31:45) and were "constructed" (Exodus 24:4; 1 Kings 14:23),

---

[3] CTA 17:1:26–30:
so that he may beget a son in his house,
a scion in the midst of his palace.
He shall set up the stela of his ancestral god,
in the sanctuary the cippus of his kinsman;

N. Wyatt, *Religious Texts from Ugarit, 2nd ed.*, Biblical Seminar, 53 (London; New York: Sheffield Academic Press, 2002), 255–256.

[4] William G. Dever, *Did God Have a Wife?: Archaeology and Folk Religion in Ancient Israel* (Grand Rapids, MI: Eerdmans Publishing, 2005), 99. "(Gen. 28:18; Exod. 24:4; Josh. 24:26–27). They are often said to be associated with a *bāmāh*, or "high place" (1 Kings 14:23; 2 Kings 18:4; 23:13–14), or a temple (2 Kings 3:2); or located near an "idol" (Lev. 26:1; Deut. 7:5; 12:3; Mic. 5:13)." William G. Dever, *The Lives of Ordinary People in Ancient Israel: Where Archaeology and the Bible Intersect* (Grand Rapids, MI; Cambridge, U.K.: William B. Eerdmans Publishing Company, 2012), 290.

"placed" (Genesis 28:18), "raised high" (Genesis 31:45), "stood up" (Leviticus 26:1; Deuteronomy 16:22), "set erect" (Genesis 35:14; 20; 2 Kings 17:10), and "artificially dressed" (Hosea 10:2).[5]

Some of these stone slabs have been found in several excavations of Israelite cities from this time period (Arad, Lachish, Tirzah, and Hazor). Five standing stones were uncovered surrounding a stone altar in the outer gate plaza of the Israelite city of Dan.[6] Standing stones could also be found in city gates. One such massebah was unearthed from the gate of the Jewish city Bethsaida. It contains an engraved image representation of a bull-headed icon of Baal.

In the Bible, Solomon was reported to have constructed sacred pillars for Baal and possibly Molech and Astarte (2 Kings 23:13-14) in the high places of Jerusalem. King Ahab of Israel is reported to have set up a pillar of Baal in the temple in Samaria (2 Kings 3:2; 10:27), as described in the novel *Jezebel: Harlot Queen of Israel*.

Zevit explains the rhetorical connection of *massebot* standing stones with the sacred tree and high place.

> Finally, there are the blanket statements about *massebot* "on every high hill and under every green tree," an expression that is often taken as a rhetorical idiom signifying "everywhere." However, as noted above in the discussion of peak sanctuaries, it most likely refers to locations of two different types of cult places. One Tyrian coin illustrates two side-by-side *massebot* under a single leafy tree while a second illustrates two *massebot* flanking a leafy tree whose branches overhang each of them.

The Bible provides no explicit details regarding the cultic rituals involved with the standing stones. But based on the Jacob narrative at Bethel, Zevit speculates that there was an intentional and silent setting up of the stone, an anointing with oil, followed by a performance declaration of promises and

---

[5] Ziony Zevit, *The Religions of Ancient Israel: A Synthesis of Parallactic Approaches* (London, Continuum, 2001), 259.

[6] William G. Dever, *The Lives of Ordinary People in Ancient Israel: Where Archaeology and the Bible Intersect* (Grand Rapids, MI; Cambridge, U.K.: William B. Eerdmans Publishing Company, 2012), 273-275.

obligations. This ritual most likely established a bond between the person and the deity, whose power allegedly indwelt the stone, as Jacob called the stone itself the "house of God" (Gen 28:18-22; 31:13). This is not equating the deity with the image, but rather the belief that the presence of the deity was within and yet separate from the stone. "Both physically and metaphysically, they represented, expressed, and guaranteed a continuous, immanent presence."[7]

The fact that Yahweh prohibited images of himself (Exod 20:4-5), yet spoke positively of pillars for Yahweh (Isaiah 19:19) while condemning pagan pillars to other gods (Exod 23:24; 34:13), suggests that pillars for Yahweh didn't have images on them, but rather represented Yahweh's presence in the abstract as a boundary marker or memorial.

Once the house of God was completed in Jerusalem from the time of Solomon onward, it would seem even properly crafted pillars for Yahweh were no longer acceptable since Yahweh claimed his house was on Mount Zion alone.

> Psalm 132:13:
> For the LORD has chosen Zion; he has desired it for his dwelling place.

> Psalm 87:2:
> The LORD loves the gates of Zion more than all the dwelling places of Jacob.

Masks

I describe the use of masks in a Tyrian ritual of Astarte worship in *Jezebel: Harlot Queen of Israel*. This wasn't an element of creative license. It was based upon a fascinating discovery of the use of masks in religious ritual on the island of Cyprus, a Phoenician colony like Tyre. As it happens, the temple of Astarte in Kition was the most dominant on the island and provided a plethora of mask artifacts for consideration.

---

[7] Zevit, *The Religions of Ancient Israel*, 260-261.

The Spiritual World of Jezebel and Elijah

Scholar Erin Averett examined the masks, which consisted of both animal and human faces: "Bull, lion, horse, stag, also monsters, cattle skulls."[8] She concluded several purposes for them. Some were used as magical devices ("apotropaic ") in graves to scare away the spirits. But they were also used by royal and priestly elite in libation ceremonies as well as "religious rituals designed to showcase their privileged access to the divine realm, legitimizing their sacred authority."[9] The context and types of Cypriot masks seem to reflect the patterns of masked initiation rites into secret societies of restricted membership.

One possible interpretation of an inscription found on a limestone tablet from Kition may indicate temple ministers wore animal costumes in the cult of Astarte.[10]

Though the precise nature of their usage is unclear, Averett concludes that these religious masks …

> … play a social role by identifying maskers with high profile ritual performances. Thus, individuals or groups became associated with divinities as attendant figures in rituals, which in turn provided these maskers with divine protection and the power and characteristics of the deity… masks thus become visual manifestations of rituals that affirm existing power structures. As multimedia public events, religious ceremonies established and confirmed social structures through the use of monumental architecture, sacred space, and symbolic objects.

Qedeshim

One of the cultic functionaries in high places and temples that appear throughout the novel *Jezebel* are the *qedeshim*, a Hebrew word somewhat

---

[8] Erin Walcek Averett, "Masks and Ritual Performance on the Island of Cyprus," *American Journal of Archaeology*, Vol. 119, No. 1 (January 2015), 12.

[9] Averett, "Masks and Ritual," 12.

[10] Averett, "Masks and Ritual," 21.

ambiguous and undetermined in meaning, though some Bible translations render it as male or female cult prostitutes (male: *qedesh*; female: *qedesha*). The word "cult" means used in sacred service or worship of a deity.

In the Bible, it isn't entirely clear exactly what the responsibilities of the qedeshim are. But some things can be surmised from the few passages where the term appears. Its first occurrence is in Genesis 32 where Judah has sexual relations with his daughter-in-law Tamar, who is disguised as a prostitute or *zonah* (v. 15). When he returns to pay her with a pledge (v. 18), he asks, "Where is the cult prostitute (*qedesha*)?" Two words used of the same woman having paid sex with Judah. So what's the difference? Deuteronomy spells it out.

> Deuteronomy 23:17–18:
> None of the daughters of Israel shall be a cult prostitute [*qedesha*], and none of the sons of Israel shall be a cult prostitute [*qedesh*]. You shall not bring the fee of a prostitute [*zonah*] or the wages of a dog into the house of the LORD your God in payment for any vow, for both of these are an abomination to the LORD your God.

From these two passages, there seems to be a difference between a normal prostitute (*zonah*) and a cultic prostitute (*qedesha*), where the qedesha is tied directly to the temple and the zonah is most likely not. Another passage in Hosea affirms this separation of secular and sacred prostitution when the prophet declares, "for the men themselves go aside with prostitutes (*zonah*) and sacrifice with cult prostitutes (*qedeshot*)" (Hosea 4:14), again delineating secular from sacred prostitution. Amos described sacred prostitution that occurred "beside altars on garments taken in pledge" also connected to temples (Amos 2:7-8).

During the time period of my novel in the ninth century, there were special rooms set aside for male prostitutes in the Jerusalem temple (2 Kings 23:7). Shocking, but true. The priesthood of the holy temple of Yahweh in Jerusalem had prostitution within its walls for much of its existence.

But what exactly were the temple duties of qedeshim? The Bible is not explicit. Karel van der Toorn has argued that it was a common custom of Israelite women to make good on unpaid vows to God by means of prostitution for the temple. A citizen would go to the temple or high place, engage the services of the qedeshim, whose wages would then go into the temple treasury as payment for the Israelite's vow.[11] Though this sacred prostitution is prohibited by Yahweh in the Torah at Sinai (Deuteronomy 23:17-18), it clearly went on with impunity for hundreds of years in the temple of Jerusalem and on "every high hill and under every green tree."[12]

Ugaritic literature describes qedeshim like those in Tyre with a bit more detail. Since the story of Ahab and Jezebel describes the cross-fertilization of Israel with Canaanite customs, it wouldn't be inappropriate to assume parallels in purpose between the two cultures. In Tyre, the qedeshim included non-priestly personnel of the temple dedicated to the deity who performed menial tasks in the temple as well as sexual activities. The Israelites most likely engaged their qedeshim in like manner.[13] Raphael Patai explains the possible functions of qedeshim:

> The function of the qedeshim had something to do with the fertility cult centering in the figure of the mother-goddess Asherah. Possibly, their services were made use of by childless women who visited the sanctuary in order to become pregnant. Such pilgrimages to holy places for the purpose of removing the curse of barrenness have remained an important feature of popular religion down to the present day among Moslems, Jews, and Christians alike in all parts of the Middle East. The qedeshim may have also functioned in rites of imitative magic in the fertility cult, whose purpose was to ensure fruitfulness in nature, the coming of the autumn rains, the growth of the crops, the multiplication of domestic animals, etc. Fertility goddesses had male attendants or priests in ancient Near Eastern religions, and in

---

[11] "The phenomenon of women—and, occasionally, men—prostituting themselves in order to obtain the money to fulfill their vows was known and to some extent accepted in broad layers of the Israelite society. Until the Deuteronomic reform, it seems to have been tolerated by the official religion."
Karel Van Der Toorn, "Female Prostitution in Payment of Vows in Ancient Israel," *Journal of Biblical Literature* 108 (1989): 201.

[12] See: Isaiah 57:5; Jeremiah 2:20; 3:6-9; and 1 Kings 14:24; 15:12; 22:46; 2 Kings 23:7; Job 36:14; Hosea 4:14.

[13] Karel van der Toorn, "Prostitution: Cultic Prostitution," ed. David Noel Freedman, *The Anchor Yale Bible Dictionary* (New York: Doubleday, 1992), 511.

the case of the qedeshim in the Jerusalem Temple, one of their tasks seems to have been to supervise the work of the women weaving linens for Asherah, which, therefore, was done in the chambers of the qedeshim.[14]

Sacred Marriage

A religious sexual ritual that shows up in *Jezebel: Harlot Queen of Israel* is Sacred Marriage. The religious rite has its origins thousands of years earlier in ancient Sumer. It was called "heiros-gamos" in Greek, and it usually occurred at the New Year's celebration. In it, the king would "marry" the goddess of fertility Inanna (later, Ishtar) in a ritual ceremony wherein he would consummate the marriage by having sexual intercourse with a priestess of Inanna as surrogate.[15] This was a cultic drama that performed the mythical love-song cycle of Inanna marrying a human king, Dumuzi.[16]

The idea was that ritual enacted underlying mythology. Since Inanna was the goddess of fertility and fecundity, Douglas Frayne explains the central purpose of the Sacred Marriage rite "was to promote fertility in the land. The rationale of the ceremony was that, by a kind of sympathetic act involving the sexual union of the king, playing the role of the *en*, with a woman, generally referred to simply as Inanna, the crops would come up abundantly and both the animal and human populations would have the desire and fertility to ensure that they would multiply."[17]

As Ugaritic scholar Mark Smith defines it, Sacred Marriage was either "between a deity and a human (ritually enacted with sexual relations)" or

---

[14] Raphael Patai, *The Hebrew Goddess Third Enlarged Edition* (Detroit MI: Wayne State University Press, 1967,1978, 1990), 299, footnote 59. See also: John Day, "Canaan, Religion of," ed. David Noel Freedman, The *Anchor Yale Bible Dictionary* (New York: Doubleday, 1992), 835.

[15] Samuel Noah Kramer, *The Sacred Marriage Rite: Aspects of Faith Myth and Ritual in Ancient Sumer* (Bloomington, IN: Indiana Unversity Press, 1969), 18.

[16] Pirjo Lapinkivi, "The Sumerian Sacred Marriage and Its Aftermath in Later Sources," in Martti Nissinen and Risto Uro, eds., *Sacred Marriages: The Divine-Human Sexual Metaphor from Sumer to Early Christianity* (Winona Lake, IN: Eisenbrauns, 2008), 8.

[17] Douglas R. Frayne, "Notes on the Sacred Marriage Rite" (review of Samuel Noah Kramer, *Le Mariage sacré à Sumer et à Babylone* [rev. ed. by Jean Bottéro; Paris: Berg, 1983], *Bibliotheca Orientalis* 42 (1985), 6.

"between two deities (imitated by sexual relations between corresponding humans)."[18]

But did the Sacred Marriage continue unchanged for millennia into the time period of the Jezebel story in the ninth century B.C.? Some scholars argue that though there were changes over time, it remained in literature of the time period such as the Baal epic (KTU 1.23). In this famous text called "The Gracious Gods: A Sacred Marriage Liturgy," the high god El is described as having sexual relations with the goddesses Asherah and Anat in connection with a ritual marriage feast consisting of human royal and priestly elites. I used this actual text in the novel when Ahab and Jezebel consummate their marriage at the high place in Samaria. A high priestess then takes the place of Asherah as Jezebel is the "Womb."

> Let me invoke the gracious gods,
> Let them give a feast to those of high rank,
> in the wilderness of the end of the world.
> Greetings, king, greetings, queen, priests and qedeshim,
> El enticed his two wives,
> Asherah and goddess Womb.[19]
> Lo, this maid bows down, lo, this one rises up,
> This one shouts, "Daddy! Daddy!"
> And this one shouts, "Mother! Mother!"
> The organ of El grows long as the sea,
> Yea, the organ of El as the flood.
> The organ of El is long as the sea,
> Yea, the organ of El as the flood.[20]

Though this text is hotly debated, some scholars such as Nicolas Wyatt contend that the myth is enacted through cultic drama in the human players of

---

[18] Mark S. Smith, "Sacred Marriage in the Ugaritic Texts? The Case of KTU/CAT 1.23 (Rituals and Myths of the Goodly Gods)" in Martti Nissinen and Risto Uro, eds., *Sacred Marriages: The Divine-Human Sexual Metaphor from Sumer to Early Christianity* (Winona Lake, IN: Eisenbrauns, 2008), 96.

[19] Adapted from: "KTU 1.23: The Gracious Gods: A Sacred Marriage Liturgy" in N. Wyatt, *Religious Texts from Ugarit*, 2nd ed., *Biblical Seminar*, 53 (London; New York: Sheffield Academic Press, 2002), 325–326.

[20] Richard M. Davidson, *Flame of Yahweh: Sexuality in the Old Testament* (Peabody, MA: Hendrickson Publishers, 2007), 94.

king and priestess.[21] This is not unlike the Babylonian myth of the Enuma Elish being recited and enacted at various points during the New Year Akitu festival in Mesopotamia.

Pirjo Lapinkivi compared similar Sacred Marriage texts over five thousand years from ancient Uruk to modern India, including ancient Israel, and he concluded there was a pattern of two different traditions.

> Either we have a human bridegroom uniting with a goddess in order to bring blessings to the world and to himself, or a human bride (= human soul) who seeks union with a divine bridegroom. In the first case, the blessings can also be obtained indirectly—two deities uniting in order to bring blessings to the king (human) and the land. In the latter case, the bride is impure at first (a prostitute) but through the necessary preparations attains purity and is ready for union with the divine. The union is often co-celebrated by other people (cult personnel, scholars, or the general public), in which case the observers and devotees identify themselves with the bride uniting with the divine bridegroom.

Others disagree. But for the novel, I explored the possibilities of what this might have looked like adapted by Israel from her pagan influencers. I also drew from the ancient manuscript *The Installation of the Storm God's High Priestess* in Emar as a Sacred Marriage text enacted by Jezebel's own installation as high priestess in Tyre.[22]

---

[21] N. Wyatt, *Religious Texts from Ugarit, 2nd ed., Biblical Seminar, 53* (London; New York: Sheffield Academic Press, 2002), 324.

[22] Douglas Frayne argues that the high priestess, at her installation, would have sex with the king as a ritual impersonating the divine pair. Douglas R. Frayne, "Notes on the Sacred Marriage Rite" (review of Samuel Noah Kramer, *Le Mariage sacré à Sumer et à Babylone* [rev. ed. by Jean Bottéro; Paris: Berg, 1983], *Bibliotheca Orientalis* 42 (1985), 5–22.

The Spiritual World of Jezebel and Elijah

Family Shrines

While doing research for the novel, one of the surprises I discovered was the idea that many ancient Jews had family shrines, rooms in their homes dedicated to religious cultic practices. Archaeologist William Dever has pointed out that previously archaeologists were preoccupied with public rather than domestic architecture, which resulted in a dearth of evidence for household shrines—until recently.

Excavations of private domiciles in a dozen Israelite cities such as Samaria, Hazor, Megiddo, Beersheba, and others from the 12th to the 7th centuries B.C. have uncovered such shrines used by single families or larger family compounds. They seem to be used for private worship as needed, and women appear to have played a significant role in their operation. The depiction of these family shrines in *Jezebel: Harlot Queen of Israel* was based on these artifacts.

Dever lists the artifacts found in these shrines containing some or all:

(1) Standing stones [*massebot*]
(2) Altars, some "horned"
(3) Stone tables and basins
(4) Offering stands
(5) Benches
(6) Jewelry
(7) Ceramic vessels, many "exotic"
(8) Animal bones and food remains
(9) Astragali (knucklebones)
(10) Terra cotta female figurines[23]

The last item on the list above, terra cotta female figurines, has proven to be enigmatic, hotly debated, and highly significant in understanding the folk religion of Israelite households. Three thousand of these clay figurines from the 12th to 6th centuries B.C. have been unearthed throughout Palestine. They average six inches tall, are all female with large pronounced breasts, and

---

[23] William G. Dever, *Did God Have a Wife?: Archaeology and Folk Religion in Ancient Israel* (Grand Rapids, MI: Eerdmans Publishing, 2005), 117-118.

instead of feet, they have a pillar base, like a tree trunk. These figurines fall into two categories: those that have the female holding her breasts up and those that have the female clutching a disc-like shape in her hand.[24]

Most scholars consider these figurines to be representations of Asherah or Astarte for several key reasons. First, the females are nude with accentuated breasts, a most common way that the fertility goddess was depicted in Canaan as opposed to ordinary women. Secondly, the disc some of the goddesses are clutching to their chests bears perfect resemblance to the breadcakes that Israelites were condemned for baking for the "Queen of Heaven" (Jeremiah 7:18; 44:19).[25] Thirdly, these figurines also perfectly fit the description of *teraphim*, or household gods, that Jacob's wife Rachel had carried with her and hid under her camel's saddle when they fled Laban's household (Genesis 31:33-35). In the time of Judges, the priest Micah had both carved images and *teraphim* in his home that were portable just like these figurines (Judges 17:5; 18:17-20).[26]

Dever concludes that these terracotta figurines must be images of Asherah that were appropriated by Israelites from the Canaanite goddess. The blatant sexuality of the Canaanite imagery of Asherah was restrained and redirected to a more chaste version of Asherah as the Great Mother patron goddess of Israelite mothers.[27]

> In the Iron Age, the principal female deity was not Astarte, but Asherah. Nevertheless, these figurines are not Barbie-like dolls. They clearly have to do with reproduction: the desire of their users to be able to safely conceive, bear children, and lactate. These are in effect "prayers in clay":

---

[24] Dever, *The Lives of Ordinary People*, 278.

[25] Dever, *Did God Have a Wife?*, 176-180.

[26] One strange exception to this small portable size was the case where David's wife Michal used what must have been a life-sized teraphim to lay in a bed to impersonate David sleeping. But one wonders how she could have possibly moved some so heavy as a life-sized sculpture, unless it was made of light material rather than clay or metal or stone See 1 Samuel 9:13-16.

[27] Dever, *Did God Have a Wife?*, 187.

talismans to aid women in having children, nursing them, and rearing them through childhood.[28]

Judean tombs of these periods have also included items used for divination and "magic," including dice and sheep/goat knuckles used for casting lots, amulets, and other good luck charms considered "apotropaic" devices used to ward off evil. "Among the most conspicuous apotropaic devices in late Judean tombs are Egyptian-style glazed Bes figurines and Eye-of-Horus amulets, whose function as popular good-luck charms throughout the Levant is well known."[29]

The Eye of Horus was known as an Egyptian symbol of protection and health. Bes was an ugly Egyptian dwarf deity with a lion face, bowed legs, and sometimes depicted with an enormous phallus.[30] Though Bes was not worshipped per se, his image could be found on vessels, household items, and amulets as a means of protecting children and pregnant mothers in their childbirth.[31]

The folk religion of many Israelites included household shrines that were more like their Canaanite neighbors' religion than has previously been assumed.

Cult of the Dead

In his dissertation "Cults of the Dead in Ancient Israel and Ugarit," Theodore Joseph Lewis defines cults of the dead as "those acts directed toward the deceased functioning either to placate the dead or to secure favors from

---

[28] Dever, *The Lives of Ordinary People*, 279-280.

[29] William G. Dever, *The Lives of Ordinary People in Ancient Israel: Where Archaeology and the Bible Intersect* (Grand Rapids, MI; Cambridge, U.K.: William B. Eerdmans Publishing Company, 2012), 271–273.

[30] H. te Velde, "Bes," ed. Karel van der Toorn, Bob Becking, and Pieter W. van der Horst, *Dictionary of Deities and Demons in the Bible* (Leiden; Boston; Köln; Grand Rapids, MI; Cambridge: Brill; Eerdmans, 1999), 173.

[31] "Found in Jerusalem's City of David: The Egyptian God Bes":
https://www.haaretz.com/archaeology/MAGAZINE-found-in-jerusalem-s-city-of-david-egyptian-god-bes-1.7042407

them."[32] Such acts would include mediumship and necromancy (communicating with the dead), food offerings, libations, prayers, and various behaviors such as body modifications and self-lacerations—all activities of which the Old Testament indicated Israelites were guilty of engaging.

The following are activities that Yahweh had forbidden to the Israelites because they were part of the Canaanite abominable cult of the dead:

Cutting and shaving one's self to be heard by the dead (Deuteronomy 14:1)
Divination, conjuring, consulting spirits (Deuteronomy 18:9; Isaiah 8:19-20)
oracles from the deceased (Deuteronomy 18:9)
Food offerings to the dead (Deuteronomy 26:14)
Passing children through the fire (2 Kings 21:6)
Libations (drink offerings) and other offerings (Isaiah 57:6)
Overnight grave vigils and eating pork (Isaiah 65:4)
Cutting the body, shaving, tattoos (Leviticus 19:26-32)
Necromancy and mediums (Leviticus 20:6, 27)
Marzeah feast: eating sacrifices for the dead (Psalm 106:28)

All of these forbidden elements are portrayed in the novel, being performed by Israelites. God had commanded them not to participate in these specific Canaanite practices in order to keep them from idolatry. One could say these commands were given before the Israelites encountered the practices in Canaan. They don't indicate that the Israelites were actually doing them. Fair enough for those commands given *before* entering the Land. But a closer examination of the texts *after* Israel was already living in the Land indicate the need to reiterate the commands precisely because Israelites were engaging in these taboo practices in significant numbers. Some passages even explicitly tell us so.

Before entering Canaan, we are told that the Israelites yoked themselves to the Baal of Peor. They ate sacrifices for the dead long after Yahweh had

---

[32] Theodore Joseph Lewis, *Cults of the Dead in Ancient Israel and Ugarit*, dissertation (Cambridge, MA: Harvard University, 1986), 282.

commanded them not to (Psalm 106:28). This was most likely a reference to the marzeah feast, which we will address later.

By the time of King Saul, Israel must have been full of necromancers because Saul had to go to great effort to "expel the mediums and the necromancers out of the land" (1 Samuel 28:3).

Absalom erected a pillar (*massebah*) in his own memory (2 Samuel 18:18), similar to the Canaanite setting up of pillars to invoke the names of their divine ancestors (CTA 17.1.27).[33]

King Manasseh of Judah, who reigned from 697 B.C. to 643, was condemned for burning his son in fire sacrifice, practicing fortune-telling, interpreting omens, and consulting the dead through mediums and necromancers (2 Kings 21:6). He reigned for fifty-five years doing this.

After Manasseh, Josiah got rid of the necromancers and mediums that had been flourishing in Judah for God knows how long. The indication in the text is that Saul's cutting off of the necromancers was only temporary in effect while Josiah's was a more thorough elimination. Which means necromancy had continued throughout the Land for those several hundred years.[34]

Two hundred years before Josiah, consulting the dead was so popular that the prophet Isaiah mocked its well-known rituals as "chirping and muttering." It was a common belief in the Near East that the dead spoke in birdlike whispers.[35] Noted Assyriologist Amar Annus explains that in the Ugaritic literature the spirits of the dead took the form of birds. "The *rpum* [Rephaim] are described as fluttering; they are startled like birds. Apparently they were believed to come like birds to the holy place to enter the company of the gods."[36]

The following biblical condemnations and mockery of necromancy now make sense in that occultic worldview context.

---

[33] Lewis, *Cults of the Dead*, 196-197.

[34] Lewis, *Cults of the Dead*, 206.

[35] "So in the Akkadian "Descent of Ishtar" (obv. 10, ANET, p. 107) and the Gilgamesh Epic (VII, iv, 38, 39; ANET, p. 87), as well as the Aeneid vi.492.3; the Iliad xxiii.101; and Horace Satires I.i.viii.40." John N. Oswalt, *The Book of Isaiah, Chapters 1–39, The New International Commentary on the Old Testament* (Grand Rapids, MI: Wm. B. Eerdmans Publishing Co., 1986).

[36] Amar Annus, "Are There Greek Rephaim?: On the Etymology of Greek Meropes and Titanes," Ugarit Forschungen 31 (1999), 15; Quoting Klaas Spronk, *Beatific Afterlife in Ancient Near East*, 1986: 167.

> Isaiah 8:19:
> And when they say to you, "Inquire of the <u>mediums and the necromancers who chirp and mutter</u>," should not a people inquire of their God? Should they inquire of the dead on behalf of the living?

> Isaiah 29:4 (NET):
> [Jerusalem] will fall; while lying on the ground you will speak; from the dust where you lie, your words will be heard. Your voice will sound like a spirit speaking <u>from the underworld; from the dust you will chirp as if muttering</u> an incantation.

In the second passage, Jerusalem is described as a city of the dead (necropolis) lying fallen in the ground, another indictment that they will become like the chirping muttering dead with whom they consult in place of their creator.[37]

Isaiah then condemns Israelites for more of their idolatry, which includes, "sitting among the tombs and keeping watch all night long" (Isaiah 65:4 NET). Most commentators have seen this as a reference to incubation rituals of all night vigils at tombs waiting for an oracle from the dead,[38] another common activity of the cult of the dead.

What did necromancy in this time period look like in the ancient Near East? The Hebrew word for a necromancer was "Ob." Cognate languages with Hebrew suggest the term *ob* was connected to …

> … a pit dug in the ground, which served as a means of access between infernal spirits of gods or deceased persons and the upper world. Among the Hittites, rituals were carried out which involved the opening up of such pits in places selected by oracle, the lowering of offerings into the pits, and the luring up of spirits out of the pit to eat the sacrifices

---

[37] Lewis, *Cults of the Dead*, 229.
[38] Lewis, *Cults of the Dead*, 244-245.

and drink the blood libations and show their favor and superior knowledge to the sacrificers.

Among the offerings lowered in the pit were foodstuffs, often including a black sacrificial animal (a hog or a dog), silver objects such as a model of a human ear (symbolizing the practitioner's desire to hear from the underworld), and a ladder or staircase (to encourage the spirit to ascend).[39]

Again, the reader will recognize much of these elements as portrayed in the novel *Jezebel*. But now let's turn to one of the strongest elements of the cult of the dead: the marzeah feast.

Marzeah Feast

One element of the cult of the dead discovered in the Ugaritic culture with corresponding echoes in the Old Testament was the *marzeah* feast, a banquet for the dead.

In Canaan and Syria, archaeological digs have uncovered special buildings outside of towns, sometimes near cemeteries, where an association of persons called "men of the marzeah" would meet for funerary meals for the dead. There is evidence of rituals performed at these locations and that deities were included in the liturgy, specifically Asherah.[40]

Ugaritic texts confirm these locations as "houses of marzeah." They were often near vineyards because the men who had special membership in the religious guild would drink wine in excess during these marzeah banquets as

---

[39] John H. Walton, Zondervan Illustrated Bible Backgrounds Commentary (Old Testament): Joshua, Judges, Ruth, 1 & 2 Samuel, vol. 2 (Grand Rapids, MI: Zondervan, 2009), 382.

[40] Manfred Bietak, "Temple or 'Bêt Marzeah'?," in *Symbiosis, Symbolism, and the Power of the Past: Canaan, Ancient Israel, and Their Neighbors from the Late Bronze Age through Roman Palaestina*, ed. William G. Dever and Seymour Gitin (Winona Lake, IN: Eisenbrauns, 2003), 165.

Also, Loren R. Fisher, *The Claremont Ras Shamra Tablets, Analecta Orientalia, 48* (Roma: Pontificium Institutum Biblicum, 1971), 46

they celebrated the passing on of their dead.[41] Marzeah is now considered to have been a well-known institution in Ugarit and most likely throughout Syria and Canaan.

Ugaritic scholar Mark Smith lists four elements that characterized the marzeah. First, it was a private association, often of members from the royal or upper class. Second, it met in a private domicile, usually the home of one of its members. Third, there was a leader of the marzeah called the "chief." Fourth, the marzeah had a divine patron, usually El, the high god.[42]

This last element of divine involvement is rooted in the possible origin of the marzeah found in the Baal epic. In the text, labeled El's Divine Feast, El invites the gods to a banquet at his house, called *marzeah* (or *marzih*). Asherah and Anat are there among others. El is described as drinking wine until he is pathetically drunk and falls on his own excrement and urine "as one dead." Asherah and Anat then go out hunting and return with an unknown cure for El's hangover.[43]

As is common in the ancient Near East, the principle of "as above, so below" applies to the marzeah. Humans have their counterpart of a human feast on earth that is based upon and indeed reflects the divine feast in the heavens. As scholar Loren Fisher explains, "El's *marzih* is a projection of the human community standing under his patronage. Presumably El's experience in his *marzih* mirrors that of his worshippers in theirs.[44]

The marzeah was mirrored in Hebrew culture as well. The biblical evidence shows a Jewish identification with the cult of the dead that is more than mere analogy.

The prophet Amos had his ministry during King Jehoram's reign in Israel just before Jehu killed the king in the storyline of *Jezebel: Harlot Queen of*

---

[41] Loren R. Fisher, *The Claremont Ras Shamra Tablets, Analecta Orientalia, 48* (Roma: Pontificium Institutum Biblicum, 1971), 45.

[42] Mark S. Smith, *The Ugaritic Baal Cycle: Introduction with Text, Translation and Commentary of KTU 1.1-1.2, vol. 1* (Leiden; New York; Köln: E.J. Brill, 1994), 142.

[43] El's Divine Feast CAT 1.114, Translated by Theodore J. Lewis in Mark S. Smith and Simon B. Parker, *Ugaritic Narrative Poetry, vol. 9, Writings from the Ancient World* (Atlanta, GA: Scholars Press, 1997), 193.

[44] Loren R. Fisher, *The Claremont Ras Shamra Tablets, Analecta Orientalia, 48* (Roma: Pontificium Institutum Biblicum, 1971), 45.

Israel. Amos gives a prophecy of Israel and Judah's ultimate exile based on their pride of entitlement and careless indulgence in apostasy. He uses the description of a marzeah banquet of celebration to condemn Israel.

> Amos 6:4–7:
> Woe to those who lie on beds of ivory
> >and stretch themselves out on their couches,
>
> and eat lambs from the flock
> >and calves from the midst of the stall,
>
> who sing idle songs to the sound of the harp
> >and like David invent for themselves instruments of music,
>
> who drink wine in bowls
> >and anoint themselves with the finest oils,
> >but are not grieved over the ruin of Joseph!
>
> Therefore they shall now be the first of those who go into exile, and
> >the revelry [*marzeah*] of those who stretch themselves out shall pass away.

The notion of marzeah feasts was so well known in Israel that God used it as a metaphor to communicate a prophecy. Israelites were like fools celebrating the legacy of the dead without realizing their own deaths were hanging over their heads. We see four of the typical Ugaritic elements of the marzeah here: eating, heavy drinking, anointing with oil, and grieving. But there is a fifth aspect included, that of laying on luxurious "beds of ivory." Ivory was a known commodity of Tyre brought to Samaria in abundance by the Phoenicians in order to upgrade the wealth status of the king's palaces (1 Kings 22:39; Amos 3:15).

While there is no mention of the Rephaim in this Amos passage, the cult of the dead does show up in a prophecy by Jeremiah that also uses assumed familiarity with the marzeah ritual within Israel.

> Jeremiah 16:5–8:
> For thus says the LORD: Do not enter the house of mourning [*house of marzeah*], or go to lament or grieve for them, for I have taken away my peace from this people, my steadfast love and mercy, declares the LORD. Both great and small shall die in this land. They shall not be buried, and no one

shall lament for them or cut himself or make himself bald for them. No one shall break bread for the mourner, to comfort him for the dead, nor shall anyone give him the cup of consolation to drink for his father or his mother. You shall not go into the house of feasting to sit with them, to eat and drink.

Jeremiah references the house of marzeah as an analogy for the death about to come upon Judah at the Babylonian exile. We read of the marzeah mourning as well as the feast of eating and drinking for consolation. But this isn't merely a generic mourning ceremony. It is the Ugaritic cult of the dead that also includes the cutting of flesh and beard that is part of the necromantic ritual of calling up the dead. This was the ritual that Anat was said to have done to herself as part of calling Baal back from the dead. It was also the same activity of cutting that the prophets of Baal did on Mount Carmel to try to call Baal back from his absence in the underworld during the drought.

This isn't to say that Yahweh approved of cult of the dead rituals. But it certainly shows that Jews were well-acquainted with such activities and were most likely engaged in them as well. Otherwise it wouldn't make sense for Yahweh to use alien liturgy against the Jews as judgment if they weren't performing that liturgy themselves. Analogies and metaphors as judgment only work if they reflect the audience's own lived experience.

The passage mentioned earlier in Psalm 106:28 about Israelites eating sacrifices for the dead at Baal-Peor during the time of Moses shows the Israelites engaging in marzeah feasts. Though the word isn't used in the biblical text, later Jewish Targums reveal that ancient Jews understood the incident at Baal-Peor to be a marzeah banquet of the dead in which the Israelites were participating.

> The MT of Numbers 25:2 reads "and they (the daughters of the Moabites) invited the people to the sacrifices for their gods and the people ate and bowed down before their gods." Targum Pseudo-Jonathan adds "and the people ate in their *mrzhn*." Similarly Sifre Numbers 131 reads "afterwards they

(the Moabites and Ammonites) returned to make for them *mrzbm*, and they (the women) invited them and they ate."[45]

The connection of the marzeah to the Baal-Peor incident by rabbinic sources also included the argument that marzeah feasts involved sacral sexual orgies.[46] The apostasy of the Israelites at Baal-Peor consisted not only of worshipping Baal, but of "whoring with the daughters of Moab" (Numbers 25:1), a sexual nuance that contextually involves more than metaphorically going after foreign gods. The Israelites were drawn to Baal through the sexual temptation of the women. Physical fornication led to spiritual fornication.

Marvin Pope has concluded, "The biblical and rabbinic correlation of the marzeah with both mourning and licentious pagan revelry may seem incongruous and even contradictory from our puritan and Victorian perspective, but not from the viewpoint of a fertility religion which recognized life and death as integral natural process and confronted death with the assertion and reaffirmation of life."[47]

The Israelites were intimately familiar with the marzeah practice of eating a banquet as a means of calling up the dead. They did it themselves. But there is another element of the marzeah that adds an even deeper element of the cult of the dead: the participation of the Rephaim. We will look at those fascinating creatures next.

Rephaim

A small corpus of tablets from the excavated Ugaritic port city of Ras Shamra are sometimes called the Rephaim Texts because of their references to the Rephaim. One of them, *A Royal Funerary Liturgy*, describes a marzeah banquet on earth that gives the order of service for the funeral of a dead king. Wyatt explains that the ritual described is the invocation of the late king's divinized royal ancestors, now called Rephaim, as part of the coronation ritual

---

[45] Lewis, *Cults of the Dead*, 146.

[46] Marvin Pope, "A Divine Banquet at Ugarit," *The Use of the Old Testament in the New and Other Essays: Studies in Honor of William Franklin Stinespring* (Durham, NC: Duke University Press, 1972), 190-191.

[47] Pope, "A Divine Banquet at Ugarit," 193.

for the new king. They were calling upon the spirits of dead warrior rulers to empower the new sovereign. It was a royal cult of the dead.[48]

In the liturgy, the Rephaim are summoned from the underworld to gather in "assembly" called "Assembly of the Didanu," which had its origins in a legendary contingent of Amorite warriors.[49] In another text, the Rephaim are sometimes translated as "netherworld shades,"[50] or "spirits like the ancient dead,"[51] sometimes as "saviors of the underworld," "eternal ones"[52] or "eternal royal princes" with armed forces.[53] They arrive on royal warrior chariots and feast for seven days.

The overall image of the Rephaim banquet is one of military action and procession. As Brian Doak concludes in his dissertation on the Rephaim,

> the rp'um [Rephaim] were indeed once thought to be heroic warriors of old, and that these figures played an important role in funerary ritual as markers of monarchic legitimation and heroic identification... dead military heroes of a period thought to be in the distant past are invoked at local cult shrines, food and drink are offered, and the hero acts in

---

[48] Dennis Pardee and Theodore J. Lewis, *Ritual and Cult at Ugarit*, vol. 10, Writings from the Ancient World (Atlanta, GA: Society of Biblical Literature, 2002), 87.

[49] Brian Schmidt, *Israel's Beneficent Dead: Ancestor Cult and Necromancy in Ancient Israelite Religion and Tradition*, Dissertation (Oxford, England, The University of Oxford, 1991), 131.

[50] KTU 1.15:3:10–19. Dennis Pardee and Theodore J. Lewis, *Ritual and Cult at Ugarit*, vol. 10, Writings from the Ancient World (Atlanta, GA: Society of Biblical Literature, 2002), 87.

[51] Brian Doak, *The Last of the Rephaim: Conquest and Cataclysm in the Heroic Ages of Ancient Israel*, dissertation (Cambridge: MA, Harvard University, 2011), 249.

[52] For example:
KTU 1.161:1–14
You are invoked, O saviours of the underworld,
you are summoned, O assembly of Didanu.
Invoked is Ulkan the saviour;
invoked is Taruman the saviour.
invoked is Sidan-and-Radan;
invoked is the eternal one, Thar.
They have been invoked, the ancient saviours.
You are invoked, O saviours of the underworld,

N. Wyatt, *Religious Texts from Ugarit*, 2nd ed., Biblical Seminar, 53 (London; New York: Sheffield Academic Press, 2002), 432–434. See also,

[53] CAT 1.22.9-10. Mark S. Smith and Simon B. Parker, *Ugaritic Narrative Poetry*, vol. 9, Writings from the Ancient World (Atlanta, GA: Scholars Press, 1997), 203.

some way—perhaps by guaranteeing fertility of land or empire, or some other status of legitimation—to benefit the supplicant.[54]

As it happens, the Rephaim are important to the biblical writers, and they appear in the Bible in one of two distinct contexts. The first is that of a race of giants in Canaan called Rephaim by the Hebrews.

> Deuteronomy 2:10–1:
> (The Emim formerly lived there [Moab], a people great and many, and tall as the Anakim. Like the Anakim they are <u>also counted as Rephaim</u>, but the Moabites call them Emim.
>
> Deuteronomy 2:20–21:
> (It is also counted as <u>a land of Rephaim. Rephaim</u> formerly lived there—but the Ammonites call them Zamzummim—a people great and many, and tall as the Anakim…

I want to draw a couple things from this introduction to the Rephaim of Canaan through Israelite eyes. First, *Rephaim* seems to be a generic description of a kind of people that are called by different names in different dialects or areas. Rephaim are called Emim in Moab. They are called Anakim in Canaan and Zamzummim in Amon. So despite the fact that Anakim, Emimn and Zamzummim were all names of people in different locations, they seemed to be interchangeable terms for a generic kind of people called Rephaim. So what kind of people were they?

The text says the Rephaim were giants, mighty warriors ("great") who were "tall as the Anakim." That height was not merely a metaphor for power but a literal reference to real physical stature. When the spies came back from Canaan, they reported the Anakim to be those who "came from the Nephilim" (Numbers 32:33). *Nephilim* in Aramaic and Hebrew literally means "giants."[55]

---

[54] Brian Doak, *The Last of the Rephaim: Conquest and Cataclysm in the Heroic Ages of Ancient Israel*, dissertation (Cambridge: MA, Harvard University, 2011), 250.

[55] Michael Heiser explains the meaning of Nephilim best here:
https://www.godawa.com/chronicles_of_the_nephilim/Articles_By_Others/Heiser-Nephilim.pdf
And here: http://michaelsheiser.com/TheNakedBible/2013/03/thoughts-nephilim-answering-criticism/

So the Anakim/Rephaim were giants from the stock of the ancient Nephilim. I explain the Nephilim and the importance of giants to the biblical storyline in my book *When Giants Were Upon the Earth (paid link)*.

Some still argue that the Bible is using size as a metaphor for greatness. But the distinction between greatness and physical size is made in Deuteronomy 1:28 and 2:21 where the Anakim/Rephaim are described as both "greater and taller than we." Yes, the Rephaim were a great people, but they were also physically tall. Hyperliteralists go too far when they claim giants twenty and thirty feet tall based on the obvious hyperbole of Amos poetically describing the Amorite Rephaim "whose height was like the height of the cedars and who were as strong as the oaks" (Amos 2:9).

Rephaim were not the ridiculous monsters of sci-fi or fantasy, rising to the height of buildings or trees. The biblical evidence indicates their size to be from seven to nine feet tall. Goliath was at most nine-and-a-half feet tall. Some legitimate biblical scholarship suggests he may have only been six-and-a-half-feet tall.[56] Because the average height of an ancient Hebrew male at this time was about 5 feet, 5 inches, that would still make Goliath a giant compared to the average man. The word "giant" simply means "unusually tall."

Goliath's brother Lahmi was as tall as Goliath because he was described as carrying a spear as large as Goliath's (1 Chronicles 20:5). Lahmi was also called a "son of Rapha," the singular word for Rephaim, that may indicate a deity behind the name and a warrior cult devoted to that deity.[57] Some English translations use the phrase "descendent of the giants" in its place.

Other descendents of the giants or "sons of Rapha" are described as being of great stature and carrying weapons that only huge men could wield.

> 2 Samuel 21:16–22
> And Ishbi-benob, one of the descendants of the giants [sons of Rapha], whose spear weighed three hundred shekels of bronze, and who was armed with a new sword, thought to kill

---

[56] Michael Heiser, "Clash of the Manuscripts: Goliath & the Hebrew Text of the Old Testament" *Bible Study Magazine Online*. http://www.biblestudymagazine.com/extras-1/2014/10/31/clash-of-the-manuscripts-goliath-the-hebrew-text-of-the-old-testament

[57] Sometimes translated as "descendant of the giants." Conrad E. L'Heureux "The yelîdê hārāpā': A Cultic Association of Warriors," *Bulletin of the American Schools of Oriental Research*, No. 221,(Feb., 1976), pp. 83-85.

> David…After this there was again war with the Philistines at Gob. Then Sibbecai the Hushathite struck down Saph, who was one of the <u>descendants of the giants</u> [sons of Rapha]. And there was again war with the Philistines at Gob, and Elhanan the son of Jaare-oregim, the Bethlehemite, struck down Goliath the Gittite, <u>the shaft of whose spear was like a weaver's beam</u>. And there was again war at Gath, where there <u>was a man of great stature, who had six fingers on each hand, and six toes on each foot</u>, twenty-four in number, and he also was <u>descended from the giants</u> [a son of Rapha]. And when he taunted Israel, Jonathan the son of Shimei, David's brother, struck him down. ²² <u>These four were descended from the giants in Gath</u>.[58]

The only other one of these "sons of Rapha" in the Bible whose actual physical height is given is an unnamed Egyptian who was seven-and-a-half feet tall (5 cubits) and carried a spear as large as Goliath's.

> 1 Chronicles 11:23
> And [Benaiah] struck down an Egyptian, <u>a man of great stature, five cubits tall [7 1/2 feet]</u>. The Egyptian had in his hand a spear <u>like a weaver's beam</u>.

A few extrabiblical sources add some more context to the size of Canaanite giants. The pseudepigraphal *Book of Jubilees*, when speaking of Og's kingdom of Rephaim, measures the giants from the size of 10 feet to 15 feet tall.

> Jubilees 29:9:
> But before they used to call the land of Gilead the land of the Rephaim; for it was the land of the Rephaim, and the Rephaim were born (there), giants whose height was ten, nine, eight down to seven cubits [10 1/2 feet to 15 feet tall].

---

[58] See also: 1 Chronicles 20:4-8.

An ancient cubit was approximately one-and-a-half-feet long. One thirteenth-century B.C. Egyptian papyrus describes Bedouin nomads (Anakim) in Canaan as being "four or five cubits (7 to 9 feet) from their nose to their foot and have fierce faces."[59]

So one context of Rephaim in the Bible is clans of very large warriors. The key to proper understanding of the word "giants" lies in realizing that our modern English notion of "giant" carries with it a bias toward our fantasies and myths of impossibly tall monsters as big as buildings. In ancient Israel, very tall people, six and a half feet and above, were considered giants, and an entire people of warrior giants had significant meaning because they represented the Rephaim warriors from the underworld on earth.

One of the most well-known biblical enemy kings of Israel was also a Rephaim giant who had a strong connection to the underworld. His name was Og of Bashan, "last of the Rephaim" who was conquered by Joshua before taking the Promised Land. Here is what the Bible says of him.

> Deuteronomy 3:11:
> For only Og the king of Bashan was left of the remnant of the Rephaim. Behold, his bed was a bed of iron...Nine cubits was its length, and four cubits its breadth, according to the common cubit.

If the size of his "iron bed" (a possible euphemism for sarcophagus) 13 and a 1/2 feet long, was an indication of his height, he would have been about nine to eleven feet tall. But there is a good scholarly argument that the bed is a literary reference to the god Marduk, whose "bed" relic in Babylon had the exact same measurements and was considered "a battle trophy and significant symbol of power...By analogizing Og's bed alongside the bed of a major deity, the author likens Og to a god and bolsters his status as a superhuman warrior. The iron material of Og's bed further emphasizes the fearsomeness of this enemy defeated by Yhwh."[60]

---

[59] Edward Frank Wente and Edmund S. Meltzer, *vol. 1, Letters from Ancient Egypt, Writings from the Ancient World, 108* (Atlanta, GA: Scholars Press, 1990).

[60] Maria Lindquist, "King Og's Iron Bed," *Catholic Biblical Quarterly* 73 (2011), 480-481.

The Spiritual World of Jezebel and Elijah

And that fearsomeness was connected with the underworld both before and after Og's death. Og is described in the Bible as living in Ashtaroth and Edrei and "ruling over Mount Hermon and all Bashan" (Joshua 12:4-5). As we described earlier, Mount Hermon was a diabolical cosmic mountain, considered ground zero for the incursion of the Watchers before the Flood. Their progeny were the Nephilim, or giants (aka *Rephaim*). We also discussed that region of Bashan as being translated as "place of the serpent" and abode of the dead. In agreement with this biblical notion, Ugaritic texts also refer to Og with the divine Rephaim and describe a Rephaim "king of eternity" who resided at Ashtaroth and Edrei, exactly like the biblical Og.[61]

In my novel, I combined this connection of Rephaim and the underworld with the other biblical oddity of a necromancer calling up Saul's spirit from Sheol. This was the kind of stuff going on in that ancient world of ninth century Israel, despite it being forbidden by Yahweh (Deuteronomy 18:10-12). The result is depicted in the marzeah feast of Ahab's death in the novel. Frighteningly and biblically possible.

But there is a problem. King David wiped out the Canaanite Rephaim giants in his days. After David, the Bible talks no more of giants on the earth. And that is why in my novel of Jezebel I don't have clans of earthly giants as I do in my series Chronicles of the Nephilim. There may be individual stragglers, but not a clan of them with any real growth of numbers.

But after the time of David, the Bible does refer to the Rephaim *in the underworld*. Rather than affirming the Canaanite notion of them as power-giving underworld rulers, the biblical authors mock those Rephaim as being powerless and weak. It's as if the Israelites were dispossessing the Rephaim in both life and literature, conquering them both on earth and under the earth.

The Hebrew word *Rephaim* is translated as "shades" or "the dead" in the few biblical cases when it is used in reference to the underworld of Sheol. While it could be interpreted as a generic reference to the souls or spirits of all dead people, there are a couple places that point to the Ugaritic notion of divinized warrior kings.

---

[61] *KTU* 1.108:1–3. See "Bashan," *DDD*, p 161-162 and Scott Noegel, "Aegean Ogygos of Boeotia and the Biblical Og of Bashan," *Zeitschrift für die alttestamentliche Wissenschaft*, 110 no 3 1998, 416.

In Proverbs 21, the phrase "assembly of Rephaim" is used in a way that seems to echo the Rephaim "assembly of Didanu," referenced earlier in the Rephaim Texts of Ugarit.

> Proverbs 21:16:
> One who wanders from the way of good sense
>   will rest in the assembly of the dead [Rephaim].

But Isaiah 14 is where the notion of mocking the Rephaim as dead divinized warrior kings comes to the foreground. The prophet is writing a condemnation of the king of Babylon. In verses 12-16, Isaiah likens that king to the Ugaritic god Athtar who sought to take the throne of Baal as the Most High god but failed.[62] As the Baal epic told the story, Athtar's feet couldn't reach the floor because he was too small to replace Baal's kingship. So Isaiah condemns the king of Babylon, using Athtar as a model, for seeking to become divinized, to "ascend to heaven above the stars of God" (v. 12) to "make himself like the Most High" God (v. 14). "But you are brought down to Sheol," writes Isaiah, "to the far reaches of the pit" (v. 15).

In Canaan, such kings when dead would join the assembly of the Didanu in the underworld as Rephaim, divinized warrior kings. But Isaiah mocks this belief. And he explicitly uses the Baal epic as his reference point.

> Isaiah 14:9–11:
> Sheol beneath is stirred up
>   to meet you when you come;
> it rouses the shades [Rephaim] to greet you,
>   all who were leaders of the earth;
> it raises from their thrones
>   all who were kings of the nations.
> All of them will answer
>   and say to you:
> You too have become as weak as we!
>   You have become like us!'

---

[62] Michael Heiser, "The Mythological Provenance of Isaiah 14:12-15: A Reconsideration of the Ugaritic Material" Digital Commons Online https://digitalcommons.liberty.edu/cgi/viewcontent.cgi?article=1279&context=lts_fac_pubs

> Your pomp is brought down to Sheol,
>   the sound of your harps;
> maggots are laid as a bed beneath you,
>   and worms are your covers.

To Yahweh, all the pomp and circumstance about mighty Rephaim ancestral kings assembling in Sheol with the ability to confer blessing, prosperity, and legitimation is so much nonsense. For they are not mighty at all. They are weak, impotent, laying in the bed of maggots and worms, unable to do anything, much less "rising" from the underworld to grant favor or power upon the living. To Isaiah, the cult of the dead Rephaim is a fraud.

So despite the fact that the folk religion of Israelites and Judahites was often deeply infected with the corruption of Canaanite practices like marzeah feasts and the cult of the dead, Yahweh and his prophets did not affirm such appropriation of paganism. They mocked it.

Child Sacrifice

Jezebel: Harlot Queen of Israel is a story about the effect of pagan Baal worship upon Israel because of King Ahab's marriage to the Tyrian princess Jezebel. One of the most serious aspects of that idolatrous religion was human sacrifice of children. Thus, the novel seeks to accurately capture what that monstrous ritual may have involved based on historical and biblical sources.

Human sacrifice is mentioned in the very first introduction of Ahab in 1 Kings 16, linking the abominable practice in some way to Ahab's influence.

> 1 Kings 16:34:
> In [Ahab's] days Hiel of Bethel built Jericho. He laid its
> foundation at the cost of Abiram his firstborn, and set up its
> gates at the cost of his youngest son Segub.

Though some believe this to be a simple reference to the builder's sons dying as a result of the reconstruction project, the language makes more sense as a reference to a common form of child sacrifice called "foundation sacrifice." As commentator DeVries notes, in this particular ritual, "the children named were probably infants, dead or alive, placed in jars and inserted into the masonry, propitiating the gods and warding off evil."[63]

Another reference to child sacrifice is in the story of Mesha the king of Moab sacrificing his son as a ritual way of warding off his enemies in battle. His enemies were the alliance of Israel, Judah and Edom in the ninth century B.C. Though this is not Israel or Judah performing the child sacrifice, it marks the reality of the activity during the same time period as Jezebel and Ahab.

> 2 Kings 3:26–27:
> When the king of Moab saw that the battle was going against him… he took his oldest son who was to reign in his place and offered him for a burnt offering on the wall. And there came great wrath against Israel. And they withdrew from him and returned to their own land.

Notice that the Israelites considered child sacrifice to a foreign god to be efficacious against them such that they withdrew. Whether or not it was truly efficacious, the ancient Hebrews certainly believed it was. They believed in the power of child sacrifice, evil though it was.

Texts from thirteenth century Ugarit were published in 1978 that detailed this exact same ritual of child sacrifice as part of Canaanite laws of holy war.

> If an enemy force attacks your [city-]gates,
> An aggressor, your walls;
> You shall lift up your eyes to Baal [and pray]:
> "O Baal:
> Drive away the [enemy] force from our gates,
> The aggressor from our walls.
> We shall sacrifice a bull [to you], O Baal,
> A votive-pledge we shall fulfill [viz.]:
> A firstborn,
> Baal, we shall sacrifice,
> A child [an off spring?]
> we shall fulfill [as votive-pledge].

---

[63] Simon J. DeVries, *1 Kings, 2nd ed, vol. 12, Word Biblical Commentary* (Dallas: Word, Inc, 2003), 205.

> A 'tenth' [of all our wealth] we shall tithe [you],
> To the temple of Baal we shall go up,
> In the footpaths of the House-of-Baal we shall walk."
> Then shall Baal hearken to your prayers,
> He shall drive the [enemy] force from your gates,
> The aggressor from your walls.[64]

Though the time period of this text is centuries before Jezebel's day, it illustrates the exact same ritual scenario that was performed in Canaanite cities until that day and after. And it was performed unto Baal.

> Deuteronomy 12:31:
> You shall not worship the LORD your God in that [Canaanite] way…for they even burn their sons and their daughters in the fire to their gods.

Child sacrifice was one of the abominable behaviors of Canaanites that was repeatedly condemned by Yahweh (Deuteronomy 12:31).[65] It was sometimes referred to directly as "burning their sons and daughters in the fire" (Deuteronomy 12:31)[66] or "passing them through the fire" (Deuteronomy 18:10 NASB),[67] and sometimes indirectly as "shedding innocent blood" (2 Kings 21:16).[68] Those innocent victims are described as food eaten by the gods (Ezekiel 23:37-39).

Unfortunately, Israelites were guilty of breaking this command of God almost immediately upon entering the Promised Land.

> Psalm 106:38:
> [Israelites] poured out innocent blood,
>   the blood of their sons and daughters,

---

[64] Alan F Segal, *Sinning in the Hebrew Bible: How the Worst Stories Speak for Its Truth* (Columbia University Press, 2012), 192.

[65] See also: Leviticus18:21; 20:2-5.

[66] See also 2Kings 17:17; Jeremiah7:31; 19:5; Ezek 16:20-21; 20:31.

[67] See also NASB95: 2Kings 16:3; 17:17; 21:6; 23:10; 2 Chron 33:6; Jeremiah32:35; Ezek 16:21; 20:26, 32; 23:37.

[68] See also: 2 Kings 24:4; Isaiah59:7; Jeremiah22:3; 26:15; Psalm 106:38.

whom they sacrificed to the idols of Canaan,
and the land was polluted with blood.

Judah was guilty of child sacrifice from the days of Solomon up to the Babylonian exile:

> Jeremiah 19:5:
> [Judahites] have built the high places of Baal to burn their sons in the fire as burnt offerings to Baal, which I did not command or decree, nor did it come into my mind—

After Solomon's kingdom split, Israel too was guilty of child sacrifice that led to their Assyrian exile.

> 2 Kings 17:17–18:
> And [Israel] burned their sons and their daughters as offerings and used divination and omens and sold themselves to do evil in the sight of the LORD, provoking him to anger. Therefore the LORD was very angry with Israel and removed them out of his sight.

Molech and his Tophet in the Valley of Hinnom in Jerusalem is the one most connected to child sacrifice in the Old Testament.[69] But he is not the only recipient of such offerings. Baal was sometimes connected with Molech as a separate but related deity. He is spoken of as being present in Molech's accursed Valley of Hinnom.

> Jeremiah 32:35:
> They built the <u>high places of Baal</u> in the Valley of the Son of Hinnom, to offer up their sons and daughters to <u>Molech</u>.[70]

Baal here could be a reference to the Canaanite deity by that name or a generic reference to "the lord" (the *baal*) of the valley area. But elsewhere, high places are linked to Baal's fertility cult, while the valley is linked to Molech's underworld cult, two distinct locations of two distinct deities.

---

[69] See Leviticus 18:21; 20:2-4; 1 Kings 11:7; 2 Kings 23:10; Jeremiah 32:35.
[70] See also Jeremiah 19:5.

Nevertheless, an interwoven connection of the two gods and their cults is expressed in Isaiah 57.[71]

> Isaiah 57:5-9:
> …you who burn with lust among the oaks,
> > under every green tree, [Baal fertility cult]
> who slaughter your children in the valleys,
> > under the clefts of the rocks…[Molech Tophet cult]
> On a high and lofty mountain [high places of Baal]
> > you have set your bed,
> > and there you went up to offer sacrifice. [to Baal]
> You journeyed to the king with oil [Molech]
> > and multiplied your perfumes;
> you sent your envoys far off,
> > and sent down even to Sheol. [valley of Molech]

The Tophet (also called Topheth) was the altar upon which children were burned in sacrifice to the deity. Everywhere the word appears in the Old Testament, it is always used in connection with the Valley of Hinnom and therefore with Molech as well.

The Valley of Hinnom, where Molech's Tophet of sacrifice was located, became "Gehenna" (a derivative of the Hebrew), a metaphor for hell or final judgment in the Second Temple and New Testament times.[72] It is a common misunderstanding to caricature Gehenna as a garbage dump. There is no textual or archaeological evidence that it was such a thing. But it was a place of evil that was judged with fire and destruction.

In Jeremiah 7 and 19, the prophet predicts judgment upon Judah because of her worship of other gods, including child sacrifice on the Tophet in the Valley of Hinnom. He prophesies that the Babylonians will come and bring great destruction upon Jerusalem. There will be so many dead lying on the ground that the name of the valley will be changed from the Valley of the Sons of Hinnom to the Valley of Slaughter.

---

[71] About Molech and Baal as separate deities see John Day, *Molech: A God Of Human Sacrifice In The Old Testament* (New York, NY: Cambridge University Press, 1989), 34-36.

[72] See: 2 Esdras 7:36; 2 Baruch 59:10, 85:13; Mark 9:43, 45, 47. See Day, *Molech*, 52.

Jeremiah 7:32–33:
… for they will bury in Topheth, because there is no room elsewhere. And the dead bodies of this people will be food for the birds of the air, and for the beasts of the earth, and none will frighten them away.

Jeremiah 19:12–13:
Thus will I do to this place, declares the LORD, and to its inhabitants, making this city like Topheth. The houses of Jerusalem and the houses of the kings of Judah—all the houses on whose roofs offerings have been offered to all the host of heaven, and drink offerings have been poured out to other gods—shall be defiled like the place of Topheth.

Yahweh says that he will turn Jerusalem itself into a Tophet of burning destruction like a sacrifice to him because of their use of the Tophet and worship of the host of heaven. This was what indeed happened when Babylon destroyed Jerusalem in 586 B.C. And thus Gehenna (the Valley of Slaughter) became the symbol of God's judgment upon those who violated his commands.

Recent critical scholarship has tried to argue that Yahweh himself actually commanded and accepted human sacrifice from Israelites and only later did post-exilic agenda-driven authors write propaganda into the Bible to try to discredit this "once-acceptable sacrifice." This is an attempt to reduce Hebrew Yahwism down to evolving Canaanite religion rather than revelation from heaven. They suggest several key passages to support this contention: 1) Yahweh's command to Abraham to sacrifice his son (Genesis 22), 2) Jephthah's vow to sacrifice his own daughter (Judges 11:29-40), and 3) Yahweh's explicit statement that he had previously commanded human sacrifice in Ezekiel 20:25.

Yahweh's command to Abraham is one of the most debated passages in the Bible. That command was clearly and contextually a testing of Abraham's faith that Yahweh didn't intend for Abraham to perform. Such hypotheticals of testing are more reflective of a contrast with the Canaanite culture than an accommodation of it. Would Abraham be willing to do what he thought was wrong if Yahweh commanded it? Abraham was supposed to trust Yahweh's righteousness and not lean on his own fallible fallen human understanding. That is a test of trust, not the validation of an evil.

Jephthah's vow has also been debated for centuries about whether or not it even referred to human sacrifice rather than a life of religious celibacy (Judges11:30). But at the end of the day, the text gives no moral judgment of Jephthah's behavior from God's perspective. Yahweh is not shown to approve of it any more than he is shown to condemn it. An argument from silence is not an argument for anything. The story merely describes what happened. Jephthah's performance of his vow thus remains to be judged by scriptural passages that do make moral judgments on human sacrifice as evil.

Ezekiel's recording of Yahweh's strange statement about statutes and human sacrifice is surely the most difficult of the passages to address. In it, Yahweh is referencing the disobedience of Israel toward him in the wilderness.

> Ezekiel 20:25–26:
> Moreover, I gave them statutes that were not good and rules
> by which they could not have life, and I defiled them
> through their very gifts in their offering up all their firstborn,
> that I might devastate them. I did it that they might know
> that I am the LORD.

It sounds as if God is saying that his laws of Torah were not good and that he deliberately defiled the people by telling them to sacrifice their children. And then he gets even more strange to suggest that this was done so that they might know that he was Yahweh. It is one list of confusing contradictions against everything else written of God's Law in the Old Testament.

The context of the passage solves the problem of misinterpretation. It wouldn't make sense that Yahweh here would say the opposite of everything he has said throughout the Old Testament about his Law. In fact, it wouldn't make sense to contradict what was previously said in *this very same chapter* of Exodus 20: that his statutes were good (v.12), that they would give life (v.11), that idols defiled them (v.7, 18), and that human sacrifice was forbidden (v.28-29, 31).

Yahweh said very clearly that regarding child sacrifice, "I did not command it, nor did it come into my mind" (Jeremiah 7:31).

Context is everything. And the context of the passage is about Israel being given over to pagan control as punishment for her disobedience. The verses before Ezekiel 20:25-26 reiterates Yahweh's warning that he would "scatter them among the nations and disperse them through the countries" (20:23-24). Yahweh gave them up to the godless nations around them whose gods they chose to worship.

Well, those gods had their own statutes and rules that violated Yahweh's law. So the best translation of v. 25 is not God "gave them those statutes," but rather as the NKJV translates, God "gave them up" to those evil laws and rules. This is what is meant by "withholding his hand" from Israel in v. 22. This is also what is meant by Paul in Romans 1 where God "gave up" the pagans to their depravity to be judged by it (Romans 1:24, 26, 28). So God gave up the Israelites to the godless nations with their godless statutes and culture that Israel was seeking after. Yahweh's goal was that Israel would suffer from her bad choices and return to Yahweh.

The attempt to attribute child sacrifice to the Bible as if it were originally a normal part of Yahweh worship has no textual support from Scripture. The fact that many Israelites engaged in human sacrifice is simply proof of what the Bible says that they were spiritually unfaithful to Yahweh for so long that he sent them into exile precisely for sins such as child sacrifice.

The obvious connection that child sacrifice has with the modern practice of abortion is not hard to catch, and thus the parallels between Jezebel's day and our own are instructive. Phrases like "sacrificing children in temples of Molech" or "on the altars of convenience" are used by pro-lifers of abortion clinics because the willing murder of one's own offspring in order to bring benefit to a person's life or to escape personal suffering is exactly what the motivation was behind child sacrifices of the ancient world. In the same way that the ancient world pleaded with the gods through child sacrifice to save them from the suffering of diseases, famine, or wars, so today's culture pleads to Molech through abortion to "save" women from the suffering of poverty, "oppressed status," or gender wars.

True believers in child sacrifice who were mothers of that ancient time considered it difficult but necessary to sacrifice their babies, just as true believers in abortion today will admit the difficulty of their act while demanding it a necessary right to sacrifice their babies. "Safe, legal, and rare" has resulted in a universal sacrament.

In the end, there is just no legitimate moral argument for murdering innocent children. And as in ancient Israel, the child sacrifice of abortion marks the beginning of the end of a civilization by the judgment of God.

Outside the Bible, child sacrifice in Phoenician culture (like that of Tyre's) has a significant presence in both textual and archaeological evidence. Among the most ancient texts that reference it are the following that wrote about the city of Carthage in North Africa, a settlement of Phoenicians.

Fourth-century BC Greek author Kleitarchos [paraphrased]:
"Kleitarchos says that out of reverence for Kronos [the Greek equivalent of Ba'al Hammon], the Phoenicians, and especially the Carthaginians, whenever they seek to obtain some great favor, vow one of their children, burning it as a sacrifice to the deity if they are especially eager to gain success. There stands in their midst a bronze statue of Kronos [Baal], its hands extended over a bronze brazier, the flames of which engulf the child. When the flames fall upon the body, the limbs contract and the open mouth seems almost to be laughing, until the contracted (body) slips quietly into the brazier. Thus it is that the "grin' is known as "sardonic laughter," since they die laughing."[73]

First-century BC Greek historian Diodorus Siculus:
"In their zeal to make amends for their omission to sacrifice the noblest children, they selected two hundred of the noblest children and sacrificed them publicly; and others who were under suspicion sacrificed themselves voluntarily, in a number not less than three hundred. There was in their city a bronze image of Cronus, extending its hands, palms up and sloping toward the

---

[73] Kleitarchos, *Scholia to Plato's Republic*, 337A: Quoted in Paul G. Mosca, *Child Sacrifice in Canaanite and Israelite Religion: A study in Mulk*, PhD Thesis, (Cambridge, MA, Harvard University, 1975), 22.

ground, so that each of the children when placed thereupon rolled down and fell into a sort of gaping pit filled with fire."[74]

Second-century AD Greek author Plutarch:
"No, but with full knowledge and understanding they themselves offered up their own children, and those who had no children would buy little ones from poor people and cut their throats as if they were so many lambs or young birds; meanwhile the mother stood by without a tear or moan; but should she utter a single moan or let fall a single tear, she had to forfeit the money, and her child was sacrificed nevertheless; and the whole area before the statue was filled with a loud noise of flutes and drums [so that] the cries of wailing should not reach the ears of the people."[75]

Though these texts speak of Phoenician child sacrifice in locations geographically removed from Canaan, they actually confirm religious and cultural connection to Jezebel's Tyre. The city of Carthage was founded by Dido of Tyre shortly after Jezebel's death.[76] As Henry Smith explains, "The evidence indicates that the Phoenicians brought this barbaric practice to Carthage from Canaan, and therefore, evidence of child sacrifice at Carthage provides evidential support for the historicity of the biblical accounts which mention such sacrifices."[77]

Critical scholars have recently sought to discredit or diminish the descriptions of Phoenician child sacrifice in both biblical and classical historians by complaining of prejudice in the authors who describe the sacrifices. In other words, biblical prophets used poetic hyperbole against polytheists, and Greek and Roman authors wrote propaganda about their

---

[74] Diodorus Siculus, *The Library of History*, Book 20, 14:4-7, Loeb Classical Library, 1954, 153. Quoted in Lawrence E. Stager and Samuel R. Wolff, "Child Sacrifice at Carthage: Religious Rite or Population Control?" Biblical Archaeology Review 10,1 (1984), 14.
https://www.academia.edu/2298111/Child_Sacrifice_at_Carthage_Religious_Rite_or_Population_Control_Biblical_Archaeology_Review_10_1_1984_30-51_with_Lawrence_E._Stager

[75] Plutarch, *On Superstition*, Loeb Classical Library, 1928, 2:495. Quoted in Smith, Jr., "Canaanite Child Sacrifice," 98.

[76] Stager and Wolff, "Child Sacrifice at Carthage, 6.

[77] Henry B. Smith, Jr., "Canaanite Child Sacrifice, Abortion, and the Bible," *The Journal of Ministry and Theology*, 93.

enemies, such as Carthage, in order to paint them as barbarians and to justify their own barbarity.[78]

But this doesn't really fit the facts. First, because authors of different eras and vastly different cultures all wrote about the child sacrifice of Carthage. That is the definition of legally sound corroborating eyewitnesses.

Secondly, both Greeks and Romans practiced infant exposure, leaving unwanted infants to die of exposure to natural elements. So they didn't condemn the killing of infants—because they practiced it. Their interest was not moral but theological.[79]

Thirdly, the archaeological evidence confirms that both biblical and classical authors knew what they were talking about. Such physical evidence of child sacrifice has been found in Phoenician colonies all over the western Mediterranean. The most famous of sites is the Tophet at Carthage, North Africa, already referenced above.

Lawrence Stager and Sam Wolff, archaeologists who had excavated the site described it this way:

> The Carthaginian Tophet is the largest of these Phoenician sites and indeed is the largest cemetery of sacrificed humans ever discovered. Child sacrifice took place there almost continuously for a period of nearly 600 years...we nevertheless estimate the size of the Carthaginian Tophet during the fourth and probably the third centuries B.C. to be, at the minimum, between 54,000 and 64,000 square feet. Using the density of urns in our excavated area as a standard, we estimate that as many as 20,000 urns may have been deposited there between 400 and 200 B.C.[80]

The excavation site involves several levels that cover time periods from 800 B.C. to about 146 B.C. Earlier dates are below the water level and not accessible. Each level consists of urns that contain the charred bones of children, both boys and girls, from newborn to three-years old, mixed in with

---

[78] Smith, Jr., "Canaanite Child Sacrifice, 93.

[79] Smith, Jr., "Canaanite Child Sacrifice, 99-100.

[80] Stager and Wolff, "Child Sacrifice at Carthage, 2.

charred bones of goats and sheep. These burnt sacrifices were made to Tanit and Baal-Hammon, the patron goddess and god of Carthage. Tanit is the equivalent of Astarte in Canaan. Some say Baal-Hammon is the equivalent of the high god El. But in Canaan Astarte was the consort, not of El, but of Baal, the "Most High." So Baal-Hammon is most likely the equivalent of the Canaanite Baal-Hadad.

Critical scholars have recently constructed revisionist theories to describe the Carthage Tophet as not being a location of child sacrifice but a cemetery for children who died of natural causes. Stager, Wolff, and Greene debunk this skepticism by explaining several aspects that mitigate such revisionary speculation.[81]

First, the natural mortality rate of children at this time doesn't match the unnaturally high mortality rate of children in the Tophet, thus indicating deliberate infanticide rather than natural causes.[82]

Secondly, none of the remains of the infants show pathological condition of disease.[83]

Thirdly, naturally expired infants are usually ritually buried in foundations of homes or near the adults of the family, not in a separate cemetery.

Fourthly, some of the inscriptions on stela above the urns describe sacrificial vows to a deity never seen in normal funerary stela.

Finally, burial urns of charred animal bones that are sacrificial substitutions are found interspersed with the children's urns, something that would only make sense in terms of sacrificial rites. There were no pet cemeteries, and animal sacrificial substitution for humans was common though not universal. Some children were still sacrificed.[84]

---

[81] These reasons were all drawn from several sources: A debate over child sacrifice: https://phoenicia.org/childsacrifice.html; Brien K. Garnand – Lawrence E. Stager – Joseph A. Greene, "Infants as Offerings: Palaeodemographic Patterns and Tophet Burial," *Studi Epigrafici e Linguistici* 29-30, 2012-13: 193-222; Lawrence E. Stager and Samuel R. Wolff, "Child Sacrifice at Carthage: Religious Rite or Population Control?" Biblical Archaeology Review 10,1 (1984).

[82] Garnand, Stager and. Greene, "Infants as Offerings, 193-222.

[83] https://phoenicia.org/childsacrifice.html

[84] Stager and Wolff, "Child Sacrifice at Carthage, 11.

Some have suggested that animal substitution evolved out of human sacrifice, but the later levels of Carthage show an increase in human sacrifice in later years, not a decrease, thus disproving the evolutionary theory.[85]

Child sacrifice was integrated into the Phoenician culture and the Israelite and Judahite cultures in a deep an affecting way. The biblical, historical, and archaeological evidence is consistent with each other.

• • • • •

If you liked this book, then please help me out by writing a positive review of it on Amazon here. That is one of the best ways to say thank you to me as an author. It really does help my sales and status. Thanks!
– Brian Godawa

More Books by Brian Godawa

See www.Godawa.com for more information on other books by Brian Godawa. Check out his other series below:

Chronicles of the Nephilim

Chronicles of the Nephilim is a saga that charts the rise and fall of the Nephilim giants of Genesis 6 and their place in the evil plans of the fallen angelic Sons of God called, "The Watchers." The story starts in the days of Enoch and continues on through the Bible until the arrival of the Messiah, Jesus. The prelude to Chronicles of the Apocalypse. ChroniclesOfTheNephilim.com. (affiliate link)

Chronicles of the Apocalypse

Chronicles of the Apocalypse is an origin story of the most controversial book of the Bible: Revelation. An historical conspiracy thriller trilogy in first century Rome set against the backdrop of explosive spiritual warfare of Satan and his demonic Watchers. ChroniclesOfTheApocalypse.com. (affiliate link)

Chronicles of the Watchers

Chronicles of the Watchers is a series that charts the influence of spiritual principalities and powers over the course of human history. The kingdoms of

---

[85] Stager and Wolff, "Child Sacrifice at Carthage, 13.

man in service to the gods of the nations at war. Completely based on ancient historical and mythological research.
ChroniclesOfTheWatchers.com. (affiliate link)

Get the novel *Jezebel* that is based on the biblical research of this book you are reading.

The Most Ruthless Queen in Ancient Israel.

Israel thought she was bringing unity, progress, and change. She brought Baal, the storm god of Canaan.

https://godawa.com/get-jezebel/

(*This is an affiliate link. I get a commission on it.*)

Great Offers By Brian Godawa

Get More
Biblical Imagination

Sign up Online For The Godawa Chronicles

www.Godawa.com

Updates and Freebies
of the Books of Brian Godawa

Special Discounts,

Weird Bible Facts!

About the Author

Brian Godawa is the screenwriter for the award-winning feature film *To End All Wars*, starring Kiefer Sutherland. It was awarded the Commander in Chief Medal of Service, Honor, and Pride by the Veterans of Foreign Wars, won the first Heartland Film Festival by storm, and showcased the Cannes Film Festival Cinema for Peace.

He previously adapted to film the best-selling supernatural thriller novel *The Visitation* by author Frank Peretti for Ralph Winter (*X-Men, Wolverine*) and wrote and directed *Wall of Separation*, a PBS documentary, and *Lines That Divide*, a documentary on stem cell research.

Mr. Godawa's scripts have won multiple awards in respected screenplay competitions, and his articles on movies and philosophy have been published around the world. He has traveled around the United States teaching on movies, worldviews, and culture to colleges, churches, and community groups.

His popular book *Hollywood Worldviews: Watching Films with Wisdom and Discernment* (InterVarsity Press) is used as a textbook in schools around the country. In the Top Ten of Biblical Fiction on Amazon, his first novel series, *Chronicles of the Nephilim*, is an imaginative retelling of biblical stories of the Nephilim giants, the secret plan of the fallen Watchers, and the War of the Seed of the Serpent with the Seed of Eve. The sequel series, *Chronicles of the Apocalypse*, tells the story of the apostle John's book of Revelation, while *Chronicles of the Watchers* recounts true history through the Watcher paradigm.

Find out more about his other books, lecture tapes, and DVDs for sale at his website, www.godawa.com.

BLANK PAGE

Brian Godawa

BLANK PAGE

BLANK PAGE

Brian Godawa

BLANK PAGE

BLANK PAGE

Brian Godawa

BLANK PAGE

BLANK PAGE

Brian Godawa

BLANK PAGE

www.ingramcontent.com/pod-product-compliance
Lightning Source LLC
Chambersburg PA
CBHW052058110526
44591CB00013B/2259